TECHNIQUES IN CLASSROOM MANAGEMENT

A Resource for Secondary Educators

Amanda M. Rudolph

Published in partnership with the
Association of Teacher Educators

Rowman & Littlefield Education
Lanham, Maryland • Toronto • Oxford
2006

Published in partnership with the
Association of Teacher Educators

Published in the United States of America
by Rowman & Littlefield Education
A Division of Rowman & Littlefield Publishers, Inc.
A wholly owned subsidary of The Rowman & Littlefield Publishing Group, Inc.
4501 Forbes Boulevard, Suite 200, Lanham, Maryland 20706
www.rowmaneducation.com

PO Box 317
Oxford
OX2 9RU, UK

British Library Cataloguing in Publication Information Available

Library of Congress Cataloging-in-Publication Data
Rudolph, Amanda M., 1973–
  Techniques in classroom management : a resource for secondary educators /
Amanda M. Rudolph.
      p. cm.
  "Published in partnership with the Association of Teacher Educators."
  Includes bibliographical references.
  ISBN-13: 978-1-57886-448-5 (hardcover : alk. paper)
  ISBN-10: 1-57886-448-8 (hardcover : alk. paper)
  ISBN-13: 978-1-57886-449-2 (pbk. : alk. paper)
  ISBN-10: 1-57886-449-6 (pbk. : alk. paper)
  1. Classroom management–Case studies. 2. High school teaching–Case
studies. I. Title.
  LB3013.R84 2006
  371.102'4–dc22   2006003115

CONTENTS

INTRODUCTION

Classroom management has long been a concern for preservice and veteran educators. Today, while education grows as a hot topic in the national news, parents and community members are raising questions about discipline in our schools. In essence, classroom management has become an issue of concern for all people involved directly or indirectly with education. As educational leaders, it then becomes our challenge to provide preservice teachers, classroom teachers, and paraprofessionals with the most effective and practical strategies and procedures for maintaining a safe, productive learning environment.

In most teacher education programs, preservice and postbaccalaureate students are required to take a classroom management course of some kind. These courses range in approach from content-based classroom management (Rinne, 1997), to routines and procedures (Wong & Wong, 1998), to crisis management (Canter and Garrison, 1994). All of these approaches offer unique and varied strategies for teachers to implement in their classrooms. This text is not intended to replace a theory-based approach to classroom management. Rather, it is hoped this book will serve as a supplement to many approaches to teaching classroom management by offering case studies that reflect common issues teachers will face in their classrooms.

PURPOSE OF THE BOOK

This book is intended to help teacher educators, preservice and classroom teachers, and administrators investigate and discuss common issues in classroom management at the secondary level. The case studies that follow will address classroom procedures, equity in the classroom, disruptions by students, rules and consequences, rewards, classroom climate, teacher-student relationships, and other problems relating to classroom management. During the course of a classroom management class, preservice teachers invariably ask: "What do I do when this happens?" The case studies in this book will depict those instances to which the students are referring. A teacher may not know how she will handle a situation until that situation actually occurs. Through the use of case studies the teacher will be able to put him- or herself in the situation and work through the options and choose the best response to the actions. In addition, the teacher will be able to talk to other professionals and compare the strategies and responses they developed.

The text is specifically geared to the secondary educator. Other books may offer case studies for elementary or middle schools, while others focus on a special population or issue such as special education or diversity. As secondary educators, we deal with older students who have unique problems and issues. Secondary educators must be able to address discipline problems that arise from social, cognitive, and physical issues.

I remember an incident that occurred while I was interning at Alamo Heights High School in San Antonio. I was teaching a political communication unit in a speech class. The students had been somewhat resistant to the content, but I pressed on. After one difficult lesson, Brian stood up and shouted, "I hate Miss Wilhite! She sucks! And I *hate her*!" as I stood there with my mouth open, and there were a few seconds of silence. And then the bell rang. What did I do? Nothing. What could I have done? A lot. Hopefully, teachers who analyze the case studies in the book will be better prepared to act.

APPROACHES TO CLASSROOM MANAGEMENT

As previously stated, the approaches to teaching classroom management range greatly. On one end of the continuum, we have authoritarian, teacher-centered approaches. At the other end, we have a laissez-faire unstructured approach, and a democratic model somewhere in the middle. In addition, the composition of classroom management courses varies within the presentation of theory and practical strategies with some classes focusing solely on the theoretical and others offering only strategies and procedures. Obviously, all of these approaches offer effective strategies to classroom management, but we also know preservice teachers are still concerned about classroom management and feel a disconnect between theory and the classroom (Smith, 2000; Love, Henderson, & Hanshaw, 1996). One way to bridge this gap is using case studies in classroom management courses.

APPROACH TO CLASSROOM MANAGEMENT PRESENTED IN THIS TEXT

Constructivism is one of the most widely embraced philosophies of education today. Many teacher education programs offer a curriculum that is based in constructivist theory. In addition, many public schools are adopting a constructivist approach to education. Basically, constructivism promotes student-centered learning with the teacher acting as a guide or facilitator as the student constructs meaning. This book utilizes a constructivist philosophy to approach classroom management.

In many college courses, students attend lectures and are assessed based on traditional tests. For a teacher to make sense of classroom management, this approach is ineffective. This book offers teachers and students a way to investigate classroom management issues and construct their own meaning. Each case study is a depiction of a classroom management problem. Readers can analyze each case study and brainstorm ideas for solutions to the situations based on any classroom management approach. The book is written to complement a vast array of discipline philosophies. In addition, it is written as a means to begin a more constructivist discussion within classroom management courses for preservice teachers. The case studies are also structured to facilitate discussion among classroom teachers, paraprofessionals, and administrators.

RATIONALE FOR CASE STUDIES

Education has utilized case studies in many disciplines for years. Medical and law students read case studies as do history, sociology, and psychology majors. And teacher education has also used a case study approach. What exactly is a case study? According to Selma Wassermann (1994), a case study scholar, cases are "complex educational instruments that appear in the form of narratives. A case includes information and data-psychological, sociological, scientific, anthropological, historical, observational, and technical material" (p. 3). In other words, a case study offers students a depiction of a real world situation in great detail. In disciplines where the ultimate outcome is to interact with another person or persons, including education, case studies can be very effective. A student is given the opportunity to explore ways to interact productively with his or her "client" when an actual interaction is not appropriate or available. In this way our preservice teachers can analyze interactions with students *before* they are actually teaching a class.

In the case of classroom teachers and administrators, these professionals will also gain insight from case studies. In the heat of the moment, a teacher has little time to think and process his or her options. A fight between students can begin in an instant. By using case studies, teachers can take time to reflect and evaluate their responses and ideas. By taking time to reflect on their classroom management practices through the use of case studies, the teachers should have effective options available to them when a discipline problem arises in class.

In addition to providing an opportunity for an authentic analysis of classroom management, case studies have many other benefits. Case studies promote critical thinking by compelling readers to dissect and think about the content of the case. Case studies can also foster collaboration among participants. In an age where time is limited, chances for professional collaboration are few. Discussions about case studies, whether in preservice education courses or staff development situations, can provide an avenue for professional collaboration and discussion. Finally, case studies also promote reflection. We are constantly looking for highly qualified teachers that continually revisit their professional growth and development. Case studies can help teachers become more reflective practitioners.

In the realm of classroom management, case studies are especially effective. Preservice and classroom teachers are both afforded the chance to analyze student behavior and their responses to such behavior in a safe controlled environment. By using case studies to learn about classroom management strategies and theories, teachers avoid the stress and tension of learning on the job, which may help new teachers stay in the profession. By discussing and analyzing, teachers will absorb effective and practical approaches to discipline problems in their classes.

CASE STUDIES AND ROLE PLAY

Case studies offer students and teachers a chance to investigate a real world situation, but adding role play to the process takes the authentic situation one step further. When a discipline problem occurs in a classroom, there are many variables that will affect the outcome of the situation. Of those variables the human factor is most important; one cannot predict another person's reaction. Case studies give teachers a chance to analyze a situation and offer insights; role play puts the teacher in the situation.

I have used role play in my classroom management courses for years and have found it effective. The education students in the class are asked to portray the teacher and students in any given situation. The students then act out the facts based on the case study and try different solutions that have been brainstormed in class. By using this approach, education students get to experience the pace and timing of situations and predict how secondary students might react to the strategies and consequences they created.

This text offers case studies for analysis. Each case study includes suggestions and tips for role playing. The primary focus of the book is to provide well-developed and practical case studies relating to secondary classroom management issues; however, role-play activities are also included and can be utilized or not.

STRUCTURE OF THE BOOK

The book is separated into three sections of case studies including: Classroom Management and Course Content, Classroom Management

and Social Issues, and Classroom Management and Special Circumstances. Each section contains five case studies relating to the topic.

Part I deals with discipline problems that stem directly from the lesson, the content, or other curricular issues. Issues addressed in this section include cheating, special needs, mixed ability classrooms, and more.

Part II focuses on the social problems students in secondary schools
face. These cases explore how various social issues can manifest into discipline problems in the classroom. Topics include popularity, racial issues, and anger.

Part III addresses the instances of aggression and violence found in
all of our schools. These case studies include topics such as violence,
bullies, and weapons.

Each case study is self-contained. The reader may follow the case
studies in succession or skip to a desired topic to study. At times, students can make teachers laugh by their misbehavior while other incidents are more serious. This book attempts to offer a balance between
the two. The case studies are intended to be practical as well as entertaining.

I

CLASSROOM MANAGEMENT AND COURSE CONTENT

Classroom disruptions arise from many different causes. However, the main cause for classroom disruptions that teachers have absolute control over is the curriculum. Many teachers view classroom management as a completely separate issue from the curriculum. The truth is that the two are inextricably tied. Teachers who practice engaging and well-planned instruction are likelier to have fewer interruptions to the class because the students are engrossed in effective lessons.

When the lesson or activity is not well planned, the students may lose interest and become confused or frustrated. When that happens, the students will find another outlet for their energy and disruption is likely to occur. When students are engaged in active learning with authentic examples and activities, they have less time to create disturbances in the classroom. A good classroom manager will acknowledge the connection between instruction and discipline.

The case studies in the following section address issues related to curriculum and instruction and how it can affect the climate and environment of a classroom. One factor that allows for misconduct is ill-planned activities or lessons that for some unforeseen reason fall short in the classroom. These ineffective lessons provide students with opportunities to disrupt the classroom. Another issue is how the content is delivered to students. Today, managing a classroom means that the teacher must adjust and adapt for the individual needs of twenty or more learners. These individual differences could lead to disruptions in the learning environment if they are not all addressed or considered in the planning and implementation of the lesson. Students will finish activities at different times, and teachers should be prepared for those students who finish work early or late. Students may also look for ways to cut corners in an assignment or lesson by cheating. Also most classrooms are now fully inclusive and the diverse population calls for different instructional and management strategies and styles. One last factor in regard to curriculum is the attitude of the students toward the subject and class. Many students may come into a classroom situation with preconceived ideas about the course or content and when those ideas are challenged, the student may resist instruction, causing a disruption in the classroom. Curriculum and instruction can be the cause of some classroom problems at times.

Overall, when thinking about ways to maintain a productive and effective classroom, it is beneficial to begin thinking about effective classroom instruction. As teachers plan more effective and engaging lessons, the students will become more interested in learning and less likely to cause disturbances in the classroom. The concepts of classroom management and instruction cannot be separated. An effective teacher thinks of both issues and plans for both at the same time.

A BAD LESSON

The environment of a classroom is affected by many variables, not the least of which is course content. As we begin to investigate the issues that influence what happens in our classrooms, course content is an appropriate place to start. The following case depicts a scenario in which course content and planning are the mitigating factors in the discipline incident.

THE SCENARIO

Mr. Bradley could hardly contain himself this morning. He knew he had a lesson that all his students would enjoy and that he would enjoy as well. He had been thinking about his eighth-grade history class and how to teach the students about the importance of the presidential election system. He wanted a lesson that would be interesting and fun for the students as they learned about the Electoral College, campaigning, requirements of the presidency, and more. He had finally decided to let the students work in groups. He knew that was a good idea; junior high students love to work in groups and talk. He knew what he wanted the students to learn so he created a few guidelines for students to use to create a presentation about a person who had run for U.S. president. Here's what he came up with:

1. The presentation should include a biography of the candidate.
2. All presentations must use a visual aid.
3. All group members must participate in the presentation.
4. Presentations should be 15 to 20 minutes long.

Mr. Bradley had also been struggling with the issue of independent learning in his classroom. He thought that the eighth-grade students should be beginning to take a more hands-on approach to their education. The presidential presentations seemed like a great time to start pushing students to take more of an active role in their learning. So, Mr. Bradley left the guidelines for the presentations intentionally vague in order to spark some creative input from the students about the project.

Mr. Bradley left the house with his bagel and coffee early Monday morning to get to school to prepare for the day. He was sure this was going to be his best lesson this year.

At 8:23 the bell rang for the school day to start. Students rushed into the building, gathered supplies, visited with friends, and headed to class. Mr. Bradley's first period American history class had 27 students in it. The majority of the students were boys because girl's athletics was also first period. That morning all 17 boys and 10 girls were there; Mr. Bradley couldn't believe his luck! Everyone began to settle down and Mr. Bradley began his lesson.

"Good morning! I am so excited this morning. We are going to start a new unit about the U.S. presidency," Mr. Bradley said. He looked around the room at all the students listening and watching.

"To give you a little background, the first U.S. president was George Washington. The Constitution includes a section on the requirements for a person to become president. Now, remember, we do have two other equally important branches of government in the United States—the judicial and legislative. But our focus for the next few days will be the executive branch or the president. Now are there any questions before I tell you about the project?"

Not one hand went up.

"Great. Here's what we are going to do." Mr. Bradley began explaining as he passed out the guidelines. "Everyone needs to join a group. In those groups, you need to pick a person who has run for U.S. president before. Then you need to create a presentation that is 15 to 20 minutes long that includes a biography. You also need to figure out what else we need to know about the U.S. president. Questions?"

Not one hand went up.

"Great! Get to work!"

No one moved for a while. Then students began to group together. The girls split off into groups of friends making three groups. The 17 boys made one group of 10, one group of five, and left two boys alone. Justin, one of the lone boys, approached Mr. Bradley at his desk. "How many people are supposed to be in a group?" Mr. Bradley looked up and saw the mess of groups.

"Hey!" Mr. Bradley yelled to get everyone's attention. "You can only have four people in a group."

Immediately, cries went up. "All you said was get in a group!" "We want to all work together!" "We can do it with ten people." After ten minutes of discussion and rearranging, there were seven groups that included all the students. Thank goodness, now they'll get to work, Mr. Bradley thought.

Mr. Bradley sat down at his desk. He was a little disappointed. He thought the students would be so excited to work in groups. He realized next time he would need to set some parameters. He looked over the class. All the students seemed to be working. At least all the groups were in a discussion about something.

Alison raised her hand. "Mr. Bradley, what are we supposed to do in our presentation?" Mr. Bradley started to answer Alison, but Morgan cut him off. "Yeah, Mr. Bradley, we don't know what we are supposed to do! When are the presentations due anyway?"

Mr. Bradley decided to address the whole class. "You guys are in the eighth grade. I think you should be able to handle this assignment. Once you decide on a person, you do some research, write a biography, and create a presentation. You get to choose what the important information is relating to that person and the presidency. You guys are kinda teaching the class. Fun, huh?"

Suddenly, Logan and Chance were standing face to face in the back of the classroom yelling at the top of their lungs. "I said our group is doing George W., you punk!" Chance yelled. "No way! We said him first. You all stole it!" Logan countered. While the boys continued to yell, Alison asked Mr. Bradley if they all had to have different presidents.

Mr. Bradley was sorely disappointed. He thought this was going to be the best lesson this year. He gave students a chance to work in groups, a chance to be autonomous, and freedom to choose a subject that interested them. Why had he failed so miserably?

BACKGROUND INFORMATION

The School

Mr. Bradley's school is a small, Southern rural school. The surrounding area is mostly agricultural and sparsely populated. The community is devoutly religious and conservative. The school is a moderately performing school meeting the standards for high-stakes testing, but not exceeding them. The population of the school consists mainly of white students from lower socioeconomic status.

The Players

Mr. Bradley is a second-year teacher. He graduated from a regional university and moved to a new town for his first job. He is young and single. He enjoys his subject area greatly and hopes to spark an interest in students to read about history and become more civic-minded. Mr. Bradley was raised in a nearby city with a large population. His parents are both college graduates. His mother works as a nurse and his dad owns a construction business. Mr. Bradley considers himself to be moderately conservative.

Logan and Chance as well as the other students in the class are very similar in background. Their families work in an agriculture field and have little or no higher education. Their socioeconomic status is lower middle class to poor. Most of the students attend church services regularly and reflect their parents' religious and political views. The area is comprised of mostly Republican supporters.

THINGS TO CONSIDER

Discussion Questions

1. Based on the case study, why did Mr. Bradley's assignment fall well below his expectations?
2. What role did the students' interest of the subject play in the failure of the lesson?
3. Mr. Bradley had great expectations for the lesson to meet the academic and emotional needs of his students. How could he have planned to better address the needs of the adolescent? What characteristics of adolescents was he trying to address? Were these appropriate to his class? His lesson?
4. There were several points in the lesson when Mr. Bradley could have salvaged the day. When were these? What could he have done differently?
5. At the end of the scenario, Logan and Chance are almost to a physical confrontation. What are Mr. Bradley's options at this point?
6. The students reflect the political views of the community in which they live. Did Mr. Bradley take these views into consideration while planning the lesson? Either way, how did these views manifest themselves during the class and cause difficulties?

Areas for Reflection

The following concepts, theories, and strategies may offer some insight into the case study. It is worth exploring the effects these ideas would have on classroom management issues.

Differentiated instruction. There has been a dramatic move to inclusive classrooms in U.S. schools. Based on this trend, teachers are trying to accommodate and instruct students of all abilities and backgrounds in one classroom. Differentiated instruction has come to the forefront as the instructional method for teaching a mixed ability classroom. Carol Ann Tomlinson (1999) states that the teachers of a differentiated classroom are flexible, use various instructional methods, allow students different ways to process information, and meet the individual needs of each learner. Obviously this approach differs from the traditional direct-instructed classrooms, and this difference will lead to differences in classroom management strategies and styles.

Content as management tool.   Research indicates that well-planned and effective instruction will lead to fewer discipline incidents (Good & Brophy, 2000; Rinne, 1997). As students encounter more engaging and authentic work, the time for off-task behavior decreases. Students who are actively engaged in the lesson have little time for disrupting the flow of the class. Rinne (1997) also suggests that teachers first use course content as a management tool. When an incident occurs, teachers should first redirect students back to the lesson or activity. Only after content-focused strategies have been attempted should noncontent strategies be implemented.

Procedures for group work.   Another strategy that may affect the classroom environment is the structure of the lesson. A great deal of emphasis has recently been placed on cooperative learning. In traditional and nontraditional classrooms, group work has been a staple of instructional strategies. However, there are effective and ineffective ways to use groups in schools. The most effective use of groups is through structured cooperative learning opportunities. Slavin (1995, p.19) states that one of the major problems that leads to ineffective group work is "diffusion of responsibility." That is, all students in the group are responsible for one assignment, activity, or artifact. To overcome this problem, he states students must all be held responsible and accountable for their learning within the group.

ROLE-PLAY IDEAS

Case Study Cast: Mr. Bradley, Alison, Morgan, Logan, Chance, two to five other students

1. Have students act out the case study with dialogue. At the end, let students brainstorm ideas for Mr. Bradley to try to defuse the

Logan/Chance situation. Then have students act out those strategies to see which is most effective.
2. In small groups, have students brainstorm ways that Mr. Bradley could have prevented the chaos in the lesson. Have each group perform its solution.
3. Have students act out the thoughts and comments of Alison, Morgan, Chance, and Logan. What were these students thinking and feeling during the lesson?

2

CHEATERS

All educational units are comprised of instruction and assessment. Just as ill-planned instruction can contribute to classroom management problems, so too can inadequate or superficial assessments. The following scenario deals with issues surrounding the role of assessment in the classroom as well as possible problems that can arise during the assessment phase of a lesson cycle.

THE SCENARIO

First period was her planning period and Mrs. Skelton was putting the finishing touches on her biology unit test. Over the past six weeks, Mrs. Skelton had covered a great deal of information on genetics. She felt her students had a really good understanding of the reproductive and genetic processes. Today she was administering the final exam for the unit.

Unfortunately, Mrs. Skelton had been ill over the past few days. (She has acid reflux and it acts up occasionally.) So, she was a bit behind in writing the exam. Luckily, she had great resources that came with the textbook. The textbook publisher sent all biology teachers who used their text a CD-ROM with a bank of test questions. Mrs. Skelton usually preferred to create her own tests, but she was in a bind and she knew the textbook publisher knew what it was talking about. She installed the CD and clicked on chapters 8, 9, and 10. Then she selected multiple-choice items and within two minutes, she had a complete multiple-choice test with 50 questions. She clicked print and headed to the copy room.

Mrs. Skelton's second period class was made up of 31 ninth graders. When the bell rang, all 31 seemed to reach the door at the same time, talking and laughing with their friends. Mrs. Skelton hated this part of the class; it took her five minutes everyday to get everyone seated, settled, and ready to work. After a lot of "shushing," Mrs. Skelton was ready to start class.

"Good morning, class," Mrs. Skelton began. "We are going to take our unit exam on reproduction and genetics today. Please get out one pencil and put the rest of your materials on the floor." Thirty-one students began moving. Eventually, everyone had a pencil and the aisles between rows were filled with books, purses, backpacks, water bottles, and such.

"All right, class. I am going to pass out the test. It is 50 multiple-choice questions and you have the rest of the period to work. When you are finished, please find something to work on quietly. Any questions?" Mrs. Skelton asked.

"Yeah. How come we have to take this test? I did not get to finish my genetic profile from last week. Can't we do that?" asked Brandon.

"We are through with all our projects for this unit. You had plenty of time to finish. It is now time to see how much you have learned," replied Mrs. Skelton. Her response met with a collective groan from the ninth graders. Somewhere in Mrs. Skelton's mind she knew that something was off; giving a test should not be this difficult. Why can't testing be easy for her?

"Okay. Everyone has a test? Great. Get to work," said Mrs. Skelton. And with that she turned around, went to her desk, and sat down.

Mrs. Skelton sat at her desk to grade papers. She also had a novel on the corner of her desk in case she finished grading before the test was over. She liked to model good reading habits for her students. As she picked up her red pen to grade, she looked over the class. Everyone was working; no one was talking. Good she thought.

After ten minutes of grading, Mrs. Skelton looked up to check on the class. Brandon was staring off into space. Javier was tapping his pencil on the desk. Jamie was putting her hair up in a ponytail. Jeanette was drinking her water. Everyone else was working.

Five minutes later. Kelly was stretching. LuAnn was sharpening her pencil. And Marie was looking at her water bottle.

Five minutes later. Everyone seemed to be working except Marie and Jeanette. Marie was handing her water bottle over to Jeanette in the next row.

Five minutes later. Mrs. Skelton was watching Jeanette and Marie very closely. After a brief look up, Jeanette gave the water bottle to Marie. Marie only looked at it as she set it on her desk. She did not drink.

Mrs. Skelton was unsettled and she decided this odd behavior warranted further investigation. She walked up and down all the aisles over books, purses, backpacks, and such. As she approached Jeanette and Marie, both girls began to work furiously. Marie slowly tried to move the water bottle to the floor. Mrs. Skelton stopped her. "Here, Marie. That's almost empty; let me throw it away." And Mrs. Skelton picked up the water bottle.

It took one glance down to see numbers one through twenty and corresponding letters.

"Jeanette, Marie, come with me. Please bring your tests," Mrs. Skelton said. All twenty-nine other pairs of eyes looked up immediately and then looked down just as quickly.

The girls stood up and followed Mrs. Skelton to the front of the classroom. "Girls, you were cheating on the test. Both of you will get zeros as your grade. What do you have to say for yourselves?" reprimanded Mrs. Skelton.

"I didn't do anything! That is Jeanette's water bottle. I didn't cheat!" yelled Marie angrily.

"Are you kidding? It was your idea!" replied Jeanette just as heatedly.

"Since neither one of you is ready to take responsibility for your actions, you can also serve one week of after school detention with me," Mrs. Skelton said.

Jeanette took a minute and decided it was not in her best interest to say anything but, "Yes, ma'am."

Marie, on the other hand, evaluated the situation differently. "I cannot do detention. I am a cheerleader. I have practice! If I don't go, I won't be able to perform! You are unfair! I didn't even do anything!" she screamed. The room was completely silent except for Marie's heavy breathing.

At this point, Mrs. Skelton realized she had a bigger problem. All she wanted to do today was give her test, do some grading, and possibly catch up on her novel. "How did an ordinary unit test end up as a total power struggle in thirty minutes?" she wondered as she reached for an antacid.

BACKGROUND INFORMATION

The School

Mrs. Skelton teaches at a new, large, urban high school in an expansive city. The school serves anywhere from 2,600 to 3,000 students in grades nine through twelve. The population of the school is culturally and economically mixed. The majority of the students are middle class, but the ethnicity of the population is balanced with no one group outnumbering the others.

The Players

Mrs. Skelton is a veteran teacher who has been teaching for 23 years. She began her career teaching science at the middle school, but after five years moved to the high school where she has been teaching biology ever since. Mrs. Skelton has always loved her content area and is proud of the time she takes to create meaningful lessons in biology. She has also enjoyed the interactions with high school students, but lately she has been wondering about her students. Five or ten years ago, students seemed to be more well mannered and conscientious. Sometimes, she does not know what is going on with today's students. In the past year or so, she has begun to think about retiring.

Jeanette is a bright girl who comes from a middle-class family. Her parents both work at the hospital. She has two younger brothers. She has plans to go to college and then medical school. Being smart is

Jeanette's major attribute. She is thought to be a nerd in some circles. Marie reached out to Jeanette in biology and Jeanette felt close to the popular students for the first time.

Marie is a cheerleader from a middle-class family. Her parents are divorced and she lives with her mother who is an office manager for a real estate company. She sees her dad every weekend. Marie is an only child. She does fairly well in school, but is not intrinsically motivated. She makes the grades so she can be a cheerleader and participate in other extracurricular activities. Right now, Marie does not have any clear plans for the future.

THINGS TO CONSIDER

Discussion Questions

1. In most instructional units, the teacher will want to evaluate the students in a summative assessment. In a traditional pencil and paper assessment, what are the strategies that can be used to ensure an effective testing situation?
2. How does the use of a prepackaged test influence the environment of the classroom? Will the students respond differently to a textbook publisher test versus a teacher-made test?
3. One of Mrs. Skelton's problems in this case was the lack of established consequences for cheating in her classroom. What are some possible rules and consequences for cheating? How can these be effectively implemented in a classroom?
4. More than likely all teachers will deal with an incident of cheating over the course of their careers. In this instance, Mrs. Skelton is unable to quickly resolve the situation before it escalates. What could Mrs. Skelton have done to prevent the final scene in this case? If she had done nothing differently, what are her options at the end of the case?
5. Obviously, the role of course content in this situation is important. However, in this case Marie has her academic performance tied to social outcomes. What are some ways for Mrs. Skelton to begin to wean Marie of social rewards and move her to become intrinsically motivated to learn?

Areas for Reflection

The following concepts, theories, and strategies may offer some insight into the case study. It is worth exploring the effects these ideas would have on classroom management issues.

Classroom policies. The most effective classrooms have established rules and procedures. Wong and Wong (1998) maintain that an effective classroom has posted rules and logical consequences for breaking those rules as well as established classroom procedures. They also purport there are two main issues regarding classroom management procedures. One, there should be a rule about academic honesty and clear consequences for violating that rule. Two, the teacher should establish procedures for taking a test in the classroom. These simple classroom policies, if designed before class begins and explained to students at the beginning of the year, can go a long way to limiting disruptions during assessment.

Alternative assessment. In today's atmosphere of high-stakes testing, standardized testing has taken the lead as the test of choice. Many teachers feel the need to prepare students to do well on benchmark tests by assessing them with traditional multiple-choice tests that mimic the high-stakes test. The downside to this trend is that teachers pass up many opportunities to use engaging and effective alternative assessments. Herman, Aschbacher, and Winter (1992) characterize alternative assessment as: asking students to perform or create, using higher level thinking skills, using meaningful instructional strategies, using real-world situations, evaluation by the teachers, and encouraging teachers to adopt new instructional and assessment roles. An assessment of this type can help students become more interested and engaged in their learning and, in turn, limits the opportunity for classroom disruptions.

Student motivation. Although extracurricular activities can be a great extrinsic motivator for student achievement, our goal as educators is to foster an intrinsic motivation for lifelong learning in our students. MacDonald and Healy (1999) offer several ways to begin developing intrinsic motivation. First, teachers can draw on student curiosity as a means to motivate. Students have a natural curiosity in the world that can be focused to a specific topic or idea. Second, teachers can use mental challenges as a means to motivate. MacDonald and Healy (1999) state that people have an innate desire to solve puzzles, mysteries, and incongruities. Third, teachers can appeal to students' needs for personal competence. Basically, students want to be good at something. As we look at our classrooms, the idea of motivation is critical. Depending on the reasons for the motivation of the students, the atmosphere of the classroom could be altered. Student motivation can play a role in averting or fostering classroom disruptions.

ROLE-PLAY IDEAS

Cast: Mrs. Skelton, Jeanette, Marie, Brandon, two to five other students

1. Have students act out the case study with dialogue. After the performance, ask students to brainstorm possible solutions to the ending. What can Mrs. Skelton do now? Have students act out the possible solutions and compare which is most effective.
2. In small groups, have students develop ways Mrs. Skelton could have prevented the situation from escalating. Have each group act out its favorite solution.
3. Have students choose to be another student in the class not directly involved in the incident. In groups of two to three, have them act out how they felt and what they thought as the class resumed.

3

A QUICK FINISH

The modern-day version of a classroom is not too different from the one-room schoolhouse except the number of students has multiplied. Many classrooms today may have close to thirty students in it, and those thirty students come with individual needs and challenges. As classroom instructors and designers, we not only need to meet the needs of all students, but also balance the time and resources we spend on whole class versus individualized instruction. The following case deals with issues of differences in students' abilities.

THE SCENARIO

Ms. Wilhite loved math. In elementary school, math was her favorite subject. In junior high and even high school, math was her favorite subject. She loved sitting in her desk working the examples in her notebook while the teacher did them on the board. She loved the order of working a problem. She like writing in pencil and she adored the square pink eraser. That's probably why she decided to be a math teacher. Her favorite daydream starred herself at a blackboard with yellow chalk and an eraser. She was born to teach math.

Ms. Wilhite had been teaching high school algebra for three years and it was every bit as orderly and rewarding as she had hoped. She had nice students who sat in nice rows. She had yellow and white chalk and erasers. She felt especially happy when she graded papers with her red pen. But lately something was amiss.

Ms. Wilhite's fifth period class, the one right after lunch, had her worried. Her students seemed to be a little unruly. Ms. Wilhite had been teaching for three years and her approach never changed. Each day, everyday, Ms. Wilhite worked problems on the board and gave worksheets or problems in the book for practice. So why should the students be unruly now when they were happy before?

Today was Tuesday and Ms. Wilhite was pondering this very issue when the students began to arrive for fifth period. As usual the students were a little rowdy after lunch. After five minutes of talking and quieting, Ms. Wilhite got the students focused and she began her math lesson. Each day was the same: Ms. Wilhite lectured for 20 or 30 minutes, walking students through the new concepts and working several examples on the board. Next, Ms. Wilhite assigned practice problems from the book or a worksheet. Today Ms. Wilhite handed out a worksheet with 20 equations on it for practice. The students had the rest of the class to finish the sheet, which amounted to 35 minutes. If they didn't finish, they had to complete the work for homework. Ms. Wilhite was not sure she was happy with this structure. After all, she had some really bright students who always finished during class and others never finished in class. Still, this was how all her math classes were taught so it must be the best way.

After Ms. Wilhite made sure all the students were working, she returned to her desk. She usually graded papers for a few minutes then began to walk around the class answering questions. Today, she had a few grades to record then she would help the students. She spent 10 minutes inputting grades into her computer grade book. As she was closing her file, she heard Joel from the back of the class. "Hey! Hey, Nelson. You got a pen?" Ms. Wilhite looked at Joel and he looked back at his desk and mumbled a, "Sorry."

By this time several students' hands were raised for help. Ms. Wilhite began on the right side of the class and started working her way from student to student.

Joel was sitting in the far left corner of the class. He could see Ms. Wilhite was busy helping other students. He had finished his work several minutes ago and was bored. He thought he might write a note to his new girlfriend, but he didn't have a pen. "Hey, Nelson. I need a pen. You have one?" Nelson handed Joel a pen.

But Joel couldn't find any paper. How could he be out of paper? He turned to his other neighbor. "Hey, Kim. Let me have some paper."

"Joel. Turn around and get back to work." Ms. Wilhite scolded.

"Yeah. Okay," Joel muttered. But he was finished and bored. He knew Ms. Wilhite kept scratch paper on her desk for students to use so he got up and started walking. Since he was up, he decided to throw away all the used paper he had found in his notebook. He stopped by the trash can. Then made his way to Ms. Wilhite's desk. Except he couldn't find the paper. So he started looking through her desk.

"Joel! What are you doing? You are not supposed to be out of your seat. You have work to do," reprimanded Ms. Wilhite.

"But I am finished. And I need some paper," Joel said.

"Get back in your seat and if you are finished, then I suggest you check your work," Ms. Wilhite said.

Joel shuffled off toward his desk. Along the way he saw Marcus drawing a really cool picture and he stopped to chat about it. Marcus had drawn the school mascot, a dragon, coming out of the side of a building. Joel was impressed. "Hey, that is really cool. You are great," Joel said to Marcus.

"Joel. For the last time get back to your seat!" Ms. Wilhite said rather harshly.

And that was too much for Joel.

"Look. I am *done* with my work. I am not bothering anyone. I just wanted some damn paper. Math is stupid and I don't see why I have to sit around here bored with nothing to do. Why can't you just leave me alone!" Joel exploded.

Ms. Wilhite was dumbfounded. Joel was one of her best students and he just yelled AND cursed at her. After a beat, Ms. Wilhite became angry. "Joel, you are out of line. Sit down and be quiet! You are disturbing the class and causing problems. Sit down," Ms. Wilhite said.

"No. I don't want to," Joel said as he headed toward the door.

Ms. Wilhite knew instinctively that she needed to do something. But what?

BACKGROUND INFORMATION

The School

The school in which Ms. Wilhite teaches is located in a small town with students from a variety of backgrounds. The school population reflects a wide range of socioeconomic levels. The ethnicity of the school population including students and teachers is mixed. There is a slight majority of white students comprising 38 percent of the school's population. The school was built in the late 1980s. The population of the school is slowly growing and will soon outgrow the building. Several portable buildings house classes. Even though the school facilities are older and limited, the school is clean and visitors can tell there is a sense of pride on campus.

The Players

As stated in the scenario, Ms. Wilhite has been teaching for three years and she has an intense love of math. She came back to her hometown to teach in the high school from which she graduated and she has been pleasantly surprised by the ways in which her former teachers welcomed her as a peer. She is especially grateful to her former calculus teacher. He has acted as her mentor since she began teaching at the school. Although she really cannot recall specifics, Ms. Wilhite remembers his class as exciting and fun. She aspires to be like him and in her heart hopes her students remember her classes as exciting and fun.

Joel is a gifted and talented student. He is from a middle-class white family who has lived in the town for generations. Joel has an older brother who is a senior and is on the basketball team. Joel is not very athletic although he is on the baseball team. Joel has an IQ of 136 and has been tracked in accelerated or G/T classes since the fourth grade. Now in tenth grade, Joel is tired of the slow pace of many of his classes, but he is also fed up with his other classes in which teachers just give him extra work. Joel's parents are very supportive and proud of him. They want him to do well in school and cannot understand why Joel comes home frustrated and unhappy and yet has straight A's on his report card. Joel has tried repeatedly to talk to his parents and teachers, but has been unsuccessful; he is at a loss to articulate what it is he really wants from school. He is becoming more unhappy and angry as the years go by. He is dreading his final two years of high school and seriously considering not attending college.

THINGS TO CONSIDER

Discussion Questions

1. Ms. Wilhite is somewhat aware that there is a problem in her class. What are possible barriers in her thinking that are keeping her from identifying potential problems?
2. Ms. Wilhite loves math and the students. Why is the love of content and students not enough to ensure a well-managed classroom?
3. How is Ms. Wilhite's approach to instruction affecting her classroom management approach? How is the structure of the class affecting the overall environment of the class?
4. Joel needed some guidance after he finished his work. Ms. Wilhite was completely absorbed helping other students with their work. What are ways she could meet the needs of both the early finisher and the average worker?
5. Joel's interruptions in class seemed to be a slight nuisance to Ms. Wilhite. However, his behavior escalated. At what point could Ms. Wilhite have intervened to avoid more disruptions? What could she have done to prevent the behavior from occurring?
6. At the end of the scenario, Joel is ready to walk out of the class. Ms. Wilhite has to act. She suddenly has a discipline problem on her hands with an audience of 30 other students. What are the possible effects of the audience on Joel's behavior? How will the audience be effected by watching the exchange?

Areas for Reflection

The following concepts, theories, and strategies may offer some insight into the case study. It is worth exploring the effects these ideas would have on classroom management issues.

Gifted and talented students.   According to the National Association for Gifted Children (2005), the definition of a gifted student is:

> Students, children or youth who give evidence of high achievement capability in areas such as intellectual, creative, artistic, or leadership capacity, or in specific academic fields, and who need services and activities not ordinarily provided by the school in order to fully develop those capabilities.

The characteristics of gifted and talented students vary. Some are academically successful; others show artistic talent, while others seem to be born leaders. The idea of gifted and talented students has expanded to include other areas of strengths like linguistics and music since Gardner (1993) introduced multiple intelligences. No matter what the area of giftedness or talent, a gifted and talented student will have unique needs in any classroom.

Differentiated instruction.   In her book *How to Differentiate Instruction in Mixed-Ability Classrooms*, Carol Ann Tomlinson (2001) states that by differentiating instruction a teacher can meet the needs of the advanced learner and the struggling learner at the same time. By differentiating instruction by ability, students begin to learn where they are ready. Tomlinson also points out that one student may be an advanced learner in English but a struggling learner in math. An important component of differentiation is assessment. Basically, the classroom teacher must constantly assess the learner to monitor his or her readiness in any given subject and then modify instruction to meet his or her needs. Differentiated instruction provides an effective strategy for managing a classroom with all types of learners.

Procedures for class work.   Wong and Wong (1998) spend a great deal of their book discussing procedures and lesson designs. First, students need to have a procedure or routine for completing work. Each student should know what is expected of him or her after completing an assignment. Second, the teacher must design lessons that address the needs of a student who finishes before the allotted time is up. Wong and Wong (1998) state that an effective teacher makes use of all possible instructional time. One of the biggest mistakes made by teachers is to have early finishers sit quietly or work on "something else." Without structure and guidance, students are left on their own, which can lead to possible class disruptions.

Coverage versus uncoverage.   In their book, *Understanding by Design*, Wiggins and McTighe (1998) discuss the idea of uncoverage. Many teachers have felt the pressure to "cover" all the material in the curriculum before the end of the year. Invariably this coverage is superficial and thin. Wiggins and McTighe define uncoverage as "inquiring into, around, and underneath content instead of simply covering it" (p. 98). Uncovering material has a sense of depth and investigation for the student. A student has a better chance of gaining ownership of the content with uncoverage rather than coverage. The ownership of and engagement with the content will decrease the possibilities for classroom disruption.

ROLE-PLAY IDEAS

Case Study Cast: Ms. Wilhite, Joel, Nelson, Kim, and two to five other students

1. Have students act out the scenario with dialogue. As the scene ends, have the student portraying Ms. Wilhite try to resolve the incident with Joel. Students can discuss whether or not the ending was effective.
2. After students discuss and reflect on the scenario, have volunteers act out possible solutions to the scenario. Debrief on why or why not the strategies were effective.
3. In a case like this, the role of the audience is important. Have students act out the scenario with a large group of students watching Ms. Wilhite and Joel. Then have them act it out with very few students watching. Did Joel's behavior change? Did the climate of the classroom change?

（4）

SPECIAL NEEDS

As depicted in the previous chapter, the mixed-ability classroom poses many instructional and managerial problems for the classroom teacher. We have looked at this issue in regard to a gifted student. However, gifted students are not the only special population included in today's classroom. Other special needs students include learning disabled, English as second language (ESL), and emotionally disturbed. In this chapter we will investigate the issues that arise while managing a classroom with learning disabled students and average students.

THE SCENARIO

Mr. Sparks teaches seventh-grade English. This is his eighth year of teaching. He enjoys the age group and has always enjoyed teaching English. This year is his first year as department chair at the junior high. He is very excited and has many ideas on how to improve the curriculum as well as instruction for the seventh graders. Four other teachers comprise the English department. They have talked about moving to a model of differentiated instruction for their department. For a test run, Mr. Sparks is trying some differentiation in his fourth-period class.

Fourth period has been a challenge this year. Mr. Sparks has twenty-seven students of many abilities and backgrounds. The class breaks down as follows: seventeen girls and ten boys—six identified special ed students with individualized education plans (IEPs); one gifted student; four ESL students; and fourteen students on free or reduced lunch. Needless to say, the diversity of his class has made meeting all students' needs a challenge. As he has thought about ways to meet the needs of his students, he also has thought about the idea of what is fair. Shouldn't all students get the same instruction and content? Isn't that fair? This idea keeps bothering Mr. Sparks in the midst of all his modifications.

Today Mr. Sparks has created a test covering adverbs and adjectives. He has spoken to the special education teacher and she approved his modifications in the test for his students. He knows he could send the students who need modifications out of the class for the test, but he thinks it is important to maintain a cohesive environment in the classroom. All six of his students with IEPs need modifications for the test ranging from more time to limited choices in answers for multiple-choice items. This is one of the first times Mr. Sparks has had to make so many modifications for one class period. He worked hard to make sure he did the best for every student; he knows he is prepared and things should go smoothly.

The bell rang for first period and the day began. Mr. Sparks administered the exam to first and second periods. Third period was his conference period and he graded the tests he has. Judging from the grades, he did a fairly good job creating the test. Scores ranged from 64 to 98. Mr. Sparks thinks that is a normal range. He had just enough time to finish his coffee and save his grades in the grade book before fourth period begins.

As usual, the students arrived in a wave of cacophony. And today they arrived with a sense of anxiety. No one likes a test and Mr. Sparks's are notoriously hard. The students settled down and waited. Mr. Sparks goes over testing procedures with the class.

"Remember everyone is to do his own work. If you are caught cheating, you will receive a zero. Make sure your answers are on the test and the answer sheet. You will have 45 minutes to finish the test. (Mr. Sparks teaches in a block schedule and 90 minutes is too long for a test.) When you are done, turn the test in to me and begin working on revisions of your patriotic essay. Any questions?"

No one raised a hand.

"All right," Mr. Sparks said as he passed out the test. "You may begin."

As each student began working on the test, Mr. Sparks went to visit each student that required modifications. He wanted to make sure they had each received the correct version of the test for their modifications. Also, he wanted to make sure Mark and Jay knew they had extra time to finish the exam. As he spoke with each student, he was reassured: Jan, Sandra, Randy, and Chuck were all working diligently and had no questions. He stopped by Jay's desk and reminded him if he needed extra time he could continue to work on the test after the forty-five minutes were up. Jay said he thought he would be done before that. Mr. Sparks stopped to talk to Mark next. Mark was still working on the first question.

"Hey, Mark. Do you have any questions about the test?" asked Mr. Sparks.

"No, sir. I'm doing okay," Mark said.

"Well, all right. But don't feel like you have to rush. You take as much time as you need to finish," Mr. Sparks said.

"Thanks. I'm okay."

And with that Mr. Sparks felt everything was right on track. He sat down to have some more coffee and check his email.

Fifteen minutes into the exam, Mr. Sparks checked the students' progress and reminded them only thirty minutes remained. He did the same at thirty minutes in, reminding them only 15 minutes remained. He warned them at 10 minutes remaining. At the five-minute warning, Kristi raised her hand.

"Mr. Sparks, can we have more time? I am not through!" Kristi asked.

Priding himself on being a fair teacher, Mr. Sparks surveyed the class to see how many students were still working. Kristi, Mark, and Sally were still working. "Kristi, most students have finished. Please do what you can and turn in your test in five minutes."

The timer went off signaling the end of the 45-minute testing period. "All right," Mr. Sparks said as he went to collect Kristi's and Sally's papers. "We need to take what we have done so far on our patriotic essays and go to our peer editing groups for feedback. You will have 30 minutes to work in your groups and . . ."

"Hey! Mr. Sparks! Mark is still working on his test! You forgot to get his paper," Kristi said.

"Kristi, I am well aware that Mark is still working. Thank you for trying to help. Now class . . ." Mr. Sparks said.

"If he can still work, I want to, too. I didn't finish my test!" Kristi complained.

Now Kristi had the attention of the whole class.

"Kristi, you need to get to work on your essay. The test is over for you."

"But, Mr. Sparks, how come he can still work on his?" whined Kristi.

"He is doing what he is supposed to be doing right now. You need to be doing what you are supposed to be doing."

"It's not fair!!!! You don't like me!" Kristi yelled.

This hit Mr. Sparks to the core. He believed he was a very fair and just teacher.

"Kristi, some people get more time to take tests for different reasons. You don't need more time. You are capable of finishing within the allotted time," explained Mr. Sparks.

Kristi stopped a moment. Then asked, "So what you're saying is if I was STUPID like Mark, I could get more time?"

Mr. Sparks was speechless. All the students looked at Mark who looked at Kristi and burst into tears. Kristi laughed.

Never in his eight years of teaching had Mr. Sparks had a situation so uncomfortable and serious. All he wanted to do was help every student. And now more students were hurt than helped.

BACKGROUND INFORMATION

The School

Mr. Sparks teaches at a small rural school outside a larger town. The school is over 150 years old. Over the past ten years, the district has seen quite a bit of growth. The middle-class parents in the town are not happy with the town's schools and have been transferring or moving into the rural school district. This influx of middle-class families has made a great impact on the school. Previously, the families of the school's students have been agricultural workers, farmers, and ranchers. Now there is a mix. In addition, the school has expanded from K–8 to K–12. Although the district now teaches all grades, the entire district is located on the same campus. Mr. Sparks has been teaching there his entire career.

The Players

As stated previously, Mr. Sparks has taught for eight years. Mr. Sparks is a hometown boy. He attended the town's school district and ran a tire shop for twenty years before returning to school to get an education degree. Like many other people, Mr. Sparks's parents discouraged him from teaching. He followed their wishes, but he was never happy running a business. After getting his degree in teaching, he knew he was right; he was meant to teach. He has a wife and two teenage daughters who are very proud of him for following his dream. He is doing what he wants to do.

Kristi is an average student who lives on a farm. The farmland has been in her family for generations. Her parents and grandparents attended the same school she does. Kristi is a member of Future Farmers of America and raises chickens for the county fair. She has a dream of one day becoming an agriculture teacher. Most of her interests revolve around her family and friends. She is not very interested in schoolwork although she maintains a B average. English is her least favorite subject. If she continues to earn decent grades and attends college, she will be the first person in her family to do so. Kristi is the oldest child in a family with five children. Needless to say, she has a great deal of responsibility at home and little one-on-one time with her parents.

Mark is learning disabled. He is the only child of two middle-class parents from town. They transferred Mark to the rural school because the student-to-teacher ratio was lower and the special education program was better. He has been attending the rural school since the fourth grade. Mark is mainstreamed for all of his classes, although he can use the special education faculty for help and resources. He usually does very well in his courses, but it takes him longer to process information. He loves English and Mr. Sparks is his favorite teacher. Mark's parents have been very conscientious in treating Mark as a normal intelligent boy; they have never considered him or labeled him as disabled. From Mark's perspective, everyone has some issue that they are dealing with daily.

THINGS TO CONSIDER

Discussion Questions

1. Mr. Sparks knew he had a diverse class from the beginning of school. How could he have prepared his class for differences in instruction and modifications from the first day of class?
2. Testing can bring up many classroom management issues. What changes could Mr. Sparks make in his testing policy to ensure a more successful testing environment?
3. Given the circumstances of the class, was Mr. Sparks's response to Kristi appropriate? Effective? How could he have responded differently?
4. At the end of the scenario, Kristi caused a major classroom disruption and Mark was crying. What can Mr. Sparks do at that juncture to rein in Kristi, comfort Mark, and reestablish his authority in the class?
5. Teaching inclusive classes with students with modifications and disabilities is especially challenging for the teacher. In order to provide the required modifications and ensure a safe environment for learning for all students, a teacher must be very diligent and proactive in planning instruction and management for the classroom. What are some strategies for managing an inclusive classroom? How can teachers establish a safe, trusting learning environment?

Areas for Reflection

The following concepts, theories, and strategies may offer some insight into the case study. It is worth exploring the effects these ideas would have on classroom management issues.

Inclusion.   The mixed ability classroom is now the norm of U.S. schools. Villa and Thousand (2003) define inclusion as "the principle and practice of considering general education as the placement of first choice for all learners" (p. 20). The wide spectrum of abilities in the inclusive classroom poses significant challenges to the classroom teacher. More and more students are being placed in the regular education classroom as their primary placement. These students have special needs ranging from learning disabilities to physical handicaps to emotional disturbances. Today's classroom teacher must meet the needs of each individual student and continue to guide the class as a unit toward knowledge acquisition and achievement.

Legal issues. The Individuals with Disabilities Education Act (IDEA) was originally passed in 1990 and amended in 1997. This act replaced the Education for all Handicapped Children Act of 1975. IDEA list six principles for educating students with disabilities:

- Free and appropriate education;
- Appropriate evaluation;
- Individualized education plan;
- Least restrictive environment;
- Parent and student participation;
- Procedural safeguards. (Ryan & Cooper, 2000)

This legislation provides schools and teachers with the legal guidelines for educating disabled students. IDEA also began the movement toward more inclusive classrooms through the requirement of a least restrictive environment.

Diversity. In his book, *Classroom Behavior Management for Diverse and Inclusive Schools*, Grossman (2004) states three competencies for classroom managers:

(1) the ability to avoid problems by having the group function smoothly without too many interruptions or disruptions and by keeping individual students involved with productive work; (2) the ability to solve the behavior problems of students who don't respond to the management techniques that avoid most behavior problems; and (3) the ability to create a classroom environment that enhances students' personal growth. (p. 4)

The last competency is especially important in the inclusive classroom. As teachers, we are not only obligated to increase the knowledge base of our students but we are also ethically bound to encourage and foster tolerance of other peoples and perspectives. America's classrooms are becoming more and more diverse year by year. Schools as social institutions will hopefully lead by example in promoting tolerance and appreciation of all people.

ROLE-PLAY IDEAS

Case Study Cast: Mr. Sparks, Kristi, Mark, and two to five other students

1. Have students act out the entire scenario. Let the actor portraying Mr. Sparks improvise a solution at the end of the scene. Have students discuss whether or not it was successful.
2. In small groups, have students brainstorm alternative endings to the scenario and then act them out. The whole group can then discuss which ones would be most effective and why.
3. Have two students perform monologues that depict what Mark is thinking as Kristi insults him in front of the class. How do the two compare?
4. Have two students portray Mark and Kristi as Kristi apologizes to Mark. Discuss the ramifications of such an apology.

A HECKLER

Although there are many normal situations in any classroom that could lead to class disruptions, there are also unusual circumstances. In the day-to-day operation of a class, a test, a poorly designed lesson, or a change in instruction could possibly lead to a disruption. On the other hand, teachers cannot always plan or control for the angry student who takes issue with a lesson or instructional method. In this case, we investigate how a student's personal preferences could lead to a problem when challenged or not met.

THE SCENARIO

She was running late this morning. Ms. Hargrove was always running late. She grabbed her strawberry toaster pastry and diet cola along with her backpack and ran into the building. Luckily, she was only late for her first-hour planning period. In addition to being late, Ms. Hargrove was also a little excited and a little anxious. Today was the day she was going to introduce the political communication unit to her speech class.

Ms. Hargrove had minored in speech in college and really enjoyed all of the classes. She could also remember what it was like to sit in a high school speech class and listen to one boring speech after another day after day. She decided to incorporate some of her favorite course-work into her regular high school speech class. Political communication seemed perfect; it was election year and the unit would coincide with the government class's unit on the election process. Her unit plan in-cluded many varied activities and assignments. Here is an outline:

1. Based on class lecture and notes, student will read and discuss var-ious famous political speeches including a State of the Union Ad-dress and Farewell Address.
2. Each student will choose one formal speech to prepare and deliver to the class as a political figure.
3. In groups of two to three members, students will create a candi-date for presidency, write a campaign speech, and present it to the class.
4. Students will take a final unit exam covering the requirements and characteristics of political speeches.

Ms. Hargrove felt that the unit was well designed. It did include a great deal of work, but it would last six weeks. And today was the day it started.

Second period started and Ms. Hargrove introduced the unit and be-gan a short lecture on types of political speeches. Everyone seemed to be very interested. Typically, Ms. Hargrove had some difficulty in en-gaging all students because the speech class was made up of students from all grades, but today, students asked questions, talked about who they wanted to run for the presidency, and formed groups. Every class was engaged and interested until sixth period.

Sixth period began like all the other classes except there seemed to be excessive whispering in the back row. Ms. Hargrove redirected the at-tention of Brian and Jeff and continued with the lesson.

"Now I am going to pass out a sheet that lists all the assignments we will have with this unit. Please remember this is a six-week unit so the work will not all be due at once and you will have plenty of time to fin-ish it," Ms. Hargrove said.

As the students read over the list of proposed assignments, the whis-pering in the back of the room resumed. This time Ms. Hargrove used proximity control to curb the behavior.

"Boys, let's focus on the lesson," she said as she walked by. And they quieted down.

As Ms. Hargrove returned to the front of the room, Brian and Jeff resumed their conversation.

"I don't know who she thinks she is or what she thinks she is supposed to be teaching, but this isn't it," Brian said.

"I know this much work is a joke. I took this class to raise my GPA. I'm not doing this crap," Jeff said.

"If Mr. Everston was here, he would not make us do it," Brian said.

Brian was referring to the previous teacher. Mr. Everston had retired last year after thirty-two years of teaching. He was one of the most popular teachers on campus even if he wasn't the most demanding. Ms. Hargrove replaced him this year in her first year of teaching. Ms. Hargrove knew that a lot of students considered speech a blow-off class, but she thought she had done a good job of rectifying that misconception. She thought there was a great deal to learn about public speaking and communication, but she also believed in a balance of work. She seldom assigned homework, but made sure students were engaged and learning everyday. She thought she had established the class as a fair, balanced, challenging, but not too demanding class. Therefore, she was unprepared and totally surprised at what happened next.

"All right, everybody. Today we began our unit on political communication. We will finish our lecture notes tomorrow and begin working in groups to create our presidential candidates. Are there any questions before the bell rings?" Ms. Hargrove asked.

Brian's hand shot up. "I want to know why we have to do this. Speech used to be a fun course and now it's not," Brian said angrily.

"Well, I think that when we get into more of the unit you will see this can be a fun topic, too. It is important for you all to understand that political speeches are created and slanted for a specific purpose and audience. I am sure you will like it," Ms. Hargrove said. She looked at the clock—three minutes until the bell rang. "Anything else?"

"She really didn't answer your question. She doesn't know what's going on," Jeff whispered to Brian.

"You know what? I've had it." Brian stood up and looked at Ms. Hargrove and at the top of his lungs said, "I hate you. I hate Ms. Hargrove. You're stupid and this class sucks!"

Brian stood there breathing hard, his face red. Ms. Hargrove was perfectly still and the class was totally silent. The clocked ticked and Ms. Hargrove glanced at the time. One minute until the bell rang. Time was about to start moving again. She had sixty seconds to fix this, but she had no idea where to begin.

BACKGROUND INFORMATION

The School

Ms. Hargrove teaches in a smaller urban school district in a big city. The district is in a very wealthy affluent neighborhood populated by doctors, lawyers, and other professionals. The city is comprised of many different ethnic groups, but the majority of the population is Hispanic. The school, however, reflects the minority of white students from wealthy families. Even though the school does not have to solve the problems associated with poverty, there are other equally important issues within the school, such as parental neglect, drugs, and suicide.

The Players

Ms. Hargrove has had to make quite an adjustment in mindset coming from a middle-class family in a small town to a wealthy school in a large metropolitan area. Ms. Hargrove graduated from a private university with a master of arts in teaching and took the first job she found. It is her first year to teach. She has always wanted to be a high school teacher. She really believes that speech class is important to all students. Although she has never suffered from the anxiety of public speaking, she realizes it is very common and debilitating for the speaker. She wants to help students feel comfortable expressing their ideas and opinions clearly and concisely to any audience. In addition, she wants students to understand that speeches can be structured to be persuasive and manipulative; she hopes to instill in her students a critical ear for what they hear on the news and from leaders in their world and towns. So far, Ms. Hargrove has been happy with her job, her class, and her students.

Brian's father is a prominent lawyer and his mother is a renowned surgeon. Brian has one younger brother in the sixth grade. His parents push both the boys to succeed and do well in school and they are expected to attend competitive colleges. Fortunately, school is easy for Brian and he is a very bright student. Unfortunately, he gets bored easily in class and maintains an air of superiority for his classmates and teachers. His disdain for teachers and teaching has caused him problems in previous classes. Right now, Brian is a junior and has one more year left in high school.

THINGS TO CONSIDER

Discussion Questions

1. Ms. Hargrove was excited and well prepared for her new unit. However, there were some issues with the unit from a few students. What are some strategies Ms. Hargrove could have used to avoid these as she introduced the unit?
2. Obviously, Brian was angry not only about the unit, but also about the course in general. What are ways that Ms. Hargrove could monitor her students' attitudes and feelings about her course? Why is this important?
3. At the end of the scenario, Ms. Hargrove has very little time to act. What are some things she could do in the time left to remedy the situation? What are possible ramifications to the class if Ms. Hargrove does nothing at this point?
4. Based on the case and the background information, what are some strategies Ms. Hargrove could use to reach Brian and help adjust his attitude toward the class? Do you think Brian will change his opinion about the course or the unit? Why or why not?
5. If Ms. Hargrove does nothing today, what would be an appropriate way to address the behavior in tomorrow's class? What would the benefits of waiting to act be?

Areas for Reflection

The following concepts, theories, and strategies may offer some insight into the case study. It is worth exploring the effects these ideas would have on classroom management issues.

Know your students.   Canter and Garrison (1994) discuss the concepts of respect, fairness, and loyalty in relationships with students. They believe that these three characteristics are critical in classroom management. A teacher should take time to nurture positive trusting relationships with students. They also state that a student who is part of a positive relationship with a teacher will feel a sense of loyalty to that teacher and, in return, the student will be more likely to behave in class and even take the teacher's side in future classroom disruptions. Teachers are the primary force in cultivating these relationships. Canter and Garrison give several suggestions for establishing rapport with students including:

- Making a point of initiating conversation;
- Monitoring and modifying your tone and body language;
- Bringing up nonacademic topics of mutual interest;
- Showing your interest and giving complete attention when students are speaking;
- Expressing care, concern, and empathy;
- Sharing appropriate personal interests and experiences;
- Smiling and having a sense of humor. (p. 17)

By no means is this list exhaustive; there are many ways to reach out to students. The key is to be sincere and maintain personal boundaries.

Differentiated instruction.   In addition to differentiating instruction by readiness and learning profile, Tomlinson (2001) also addresses differentiation by interest. According to Tomlinson there are four goals for interest-based instruction:

(1) helping students realize that there is match between school and their own desires to learn, (2) demonstrating the connectedness between all learning, (3) using skills or ideas familiar to students as a bridge to ideas or skills less familiar to them, and (4) enhancing student motivation to learn. (p. 53)

The basic idea of interest-based differentiation is to begin investigating ideas or concepts in a manner that complements what the student is currently interested in, then moving that student to a new level of understanding and comprehension using his or her interest as a means of motivation. Teachers can initiate a lesson based on individual student interest and still lead all students to the same concepts, ideas, or theories.

Authentic learning. According to Glatthorn (1999), authentic learning is "developed by working on complex problems that usually do not have a single correct answer, but instead involve multiple interpretations and explanations . . . and deal with real-life situation" (p. 27). Students are more engaged in work that has real world applications. All teachers have heard students ask "Why do we have to know this?" Authentic learning answers that question without the students even having to ask. Assignments and discussions take place in a framework of the students' world. The epitome of authentic learning is a unit or lesson that is not only set in a real world framework but will also influence or change that world. For example, a new department store is coming to town and the students are very excited. However, the building codes call for so many trees to remain in the new construction and the department store has applied for a waiver. A class can learn about economics, city government, public speaking, editorial writing, and many other topics by studying within the framework of the local hot issue.

ROLE-PLAY IDEAS

Case Study Cast: Ms. Hargrove, Brian, Jeff, and two to five other students

1. Have students act out the complete scenario with dialogue. At the end, ask for suggestions for Ms. Hargrove to try with Brian and the class. Which are more effective?
2. In small groups, have students brainstorm ways to prevent Brian's behavior. Have each group act out their best idea and discuss it as a whole class.
3. Have students act out the scenario with an alternate ending. What would happen to the class and Ms. Hargrove if Brian stormed out of the room? What would happen if Ms. Hargrove began to cry?
4. Have students act out what might happen during the next day when the class meets.

II

CLASSROOM MANAGEMENT
AND SOCIAL ISSUES

In secondary education classrooms, the students are comprised of individuals journeying through adolescence at various rates. Adolescence is a unique time in a student's life that brings with it specific social, cognitive, and physical changes. The students in the secondary education classroom are children growing steadily toward young adulthood. In any environment, the adolescent may have issues to work through, but the classroom environment can be greatly disrupted by the normal angst of an adolescent.

In the time they spend attending middle school and high school, students will face a multitude of social problems that could manifest themselves as problems in the classroom. Students at this age want to be well liked and popular. However, by the very definition of popular, not all students can achieve that coveted social status, which can lead to hard feelings and anger. Students also want attention from peers and authority figures. This can lead to attention-getting behaviors in the classroom and disruptions to the learning environment. In addition, students are vulnerable to gossip and rumors that seem to be a critical part of the adolescent social structure. All of these concepts are fairly common in the landscape of the adolescent's life, and not only are the students continually dealing with these unique social issues of adolescents but also the social issues of the adult world as well.

Students in secondary education schools are trying to form their own identities, part of which are their political and social opinions. A great deal of the time students begin by mimicking the beliefs held by their parents or other significant adults in their lives. These beliefs include ideas on politics, religion, money, race, sex, and gender. As students work through their opinions and beliefs, the teachers in the classroom must be aware of the dissonance that can be created when the views are challenged by curricula or other students. Although critical to the development of the student, this exploration of ideas can lead to anger and frustration, which in turn can cause a disruption in the learning environment. The following cases explore these concepts related to the social development and structure of the adolescent's life.

All in all, the social atmosphere of the classroom can also be a catalyst for disciplinary incidents in the classroom. Unfortunately, the teacher does not have as much direct control over this variable as he or she does with curriculum. All teachers need to be aware of the unique and individual needs of the students in their classrooms. The social growth of the adolescent student can cause turmoil in the young person's life and be manifest as a discipline problem in the class. The more teachers are aware of adolescent development and the individual needs of their learners, the better the chances are of maintaining a productive learning environment.

THE CLASS CLOWN

Not only are classroom management issues affected by the content of a course, but they are also affected by social issues of the students. Students are motivated by many factors including physical, emotional, and social needs. There are times when a classroom disruption or problem occurs that has little to do with what is happening in the class and more to do with what is happening with a particular student or students. The following case deals with the lighter side of social issues in the classroom—the class clown.

THE SCENARIO

Mr. Fields's first love was basketball. He played in high school and college. He knew he was not in line to be a professional athlete, but he just couldn't picture himself away from the game for the rest of his life. He wanted to play everyday. The most logical answer was to become a high school coach, and, for the most part, Mr. Fields enjoyed the students and sharing his passion for the game. Unfortunately, however, he did not have a great love for the regular physical education class. He knew he could not get a job solely coaching so he put up with the PE classes.

Obviously, his favorite time was when they were in the middle of the basketball unit, but he went through the motions for all the other units as well.

Mr. Fields has three PE classes of all boys. Today the boys were finishing up a fitness assessment they had been working on for a week. On Monday, they will begin basketball. Mr. Fields can't wait. All he had to do today is get times for all the boys on the 100-meter dash and the fitness assessment would be complete. The next six weeks will be a breeze playing basketball.

Mr. Fields was all set for third period when the bell rang. The cones were set up; he had his stopwatch and clipboard. Everyday the boys come in, put their books and backpacks in the bleachers, then change into gym clothes. After they change, they have assigned spots on the floor where they begin warm-ups while Mr. Fields takes roll. And today they came in like a herd of cattle. Immediately, Mr. Fields began to yell. (He had to yell to be heard over the noise of the boys.) "Get moving. Put your bags down. Get dressed. Hurry! You have two minutes!"

Most of the boys had made it to the locker room to change by now, but there was a small group straggling in. Mr. Fields noticed it is Dennis walking in slowly with a lopsided grin surrounded by three other boys. Mr. Fields really likes Dennis; he is a hard student not to like, but he does like to make the class laugh. Sometimes Mr. Fields appreciates that and sometimes it is distracting. Overall, even though he is somewhat mischievous and troublesome, Dennis is a good-natured kid. But today, Mr. Fields noticed, Dennis had his troublemaker face on.

"Dennis, get a move on. You're late. Come on, guys. Get changed," Mr. Fields said.

Dennis continued to amble into the gym. He was about ten feet away when Mr. Fields tried again.

"Boy, move it. I'm in no mood today and we have a lot to do," Mr. Fields said.

Dennis visibly paused and his lopsided grin wavered. But, by this time, the other boys were changed, out of the locker room, and warming up. A few had all ready stopped to watch Dennis. His audience was ready.

Dennis finally made his way to Mr. Fields. He was still smiling, but Mr. Fields had his hands on his hips and didn't look too happy. "Dennis, what is your problem? We have to get class started. Go change," Mr. Fields said.

"Mr. Fields, I can't. I have a slight problem," Dennis answered.

"What is it?" Mr. Fields asked, playing his part in the scene.

And at that moment, Dennis turned around and showed Mr. Fields and the whole class his back where both his hands were secured tightly in handcuffs.

Dennis was immediately rewarded with a wave of laughter that Mr. Fields silenced with a sharp look.

"That's really amusing, Dennis. Take them off and get changed," Mr. Fields said as he turned to instruct the rest of the class.

"Well, Mr. Fields, you see, I actually don't have the key," Dennis said while grinning his grin. This statement produced another round of laughter from the audience.

"What? Where is the key, Dennis?" Mr. Fields asked somewhat tersely.

"Well, you see, this guy named Darren had the cuffs in English last period and he thought it would be fun to cuff me. Well, I thought so too. But, then the dude ran off to his next class with the keys," Dennis explained.

"What class did he go to?" Mr. Fields asked a little more tersely.

"Well, I am not sure. I don't know him all that well," Dennis said.

"I suggest you find him. Now," Mr. Fields said and he turned his back to Dennis and tried to begin class.

Just as Mr. Fields was about to give instructions for the day, the loudest wave of laughter yet came washing over him from the class. Not wanting to, but having to do it anyway, Mr. Fields turned around to look at Dennis.

Dennis was on the floor wiggling around a great deal. He had his back on the floor and he was trying to squeeze his bottom half through his arms so he could have his hands in front of him. The whole process was accompanied by various grunts and groans from Dennis.

Maybe on some other day, Mr. Fields would have been amused, but today he was pressed for time and Dennis was wasting more precious minutes writhing on the floor.

"Dennis, you have until I count to five to get up off the floor and out the door to find the key," Mr. Dennis said. "One, two . . ."

Dennis started moving. He was halfway to the door when he turned around. "Hey, Mr. Fields! Look, I found the key! It must have been in the handcuffs all along," Dennis said smiling at Mr. Fields. Again, the audience roared with laughter.

That was Mr. Fields breaking point. "Dennis, give me the handcuffs, change your clothes, and start running laps and don't stop until I tell you to," Mr. Fields said.

At last, Dennis's smile faded. He removed the handcuffs, handed them to Mr. Fields, and shuffled by.

"I don't know what the big deal is. Why can't you take a joke?" he mumbled.

Mr. Fields took a deep breath.

BACKGROUND INFORMATION

The School

Mr. Fields teaches at a midsize suburban high school in a typical Midwestern town. The community is diverse, but relatively conservative. The school has tremendous support from the community; parents and businesses act as invested partners in the school and district. The school has been successful and consistently produces high-achieving students. In addition to a major emphasis on learning and achievement, the school and community are proud of their student athletes. Overall, the school offers a well-balanced positive environment.

The Players

As stated in the case, Mr. Fields was a high school and collegiate athlete. Like many other sportsmen, he has an abiding love for his sport: basketball. He was led to teaching partly because he did not want to give up his relationship to his sport, but he also has always had a desire to help nurture and support children in a positive learning environment. During college, Mr. Fields volunteered at the Boys and Girls Club as a basketball coach. He also thinks that there is a real and serious problem with obesity and sedentary lifestyles of students today. He tries to model fitness for all his students. Even though he wants to help and teach all students, it is obvious to them that his passion is basketball. Mr. Fields has been teaching for 14 years; the past four years have been at his current school.

Dennis is a tenth-grade African American boy. His parents are divorced, and he maintains a good relationship with his mother with whom he lives. Dennis's father is in the military and was away a lot when he was growing up and is still stationed rather far away from Dennis. Dennis sees his father once every six weeks or so, usually for day visits. Dennis loves his mother very much and is surrounded by caring adults from her side of the family, but he still misses having his dad in his life. His mom tries very hard to meet all of Dennis's needs, but she can't ever be a father. Dennis looks up to Mr. Fields and respects his views and opinions. Dennis even secretly dreams of making the basketball team. Dennis is known on campus for being a joker and clown. Most teachers think he just needs the extra attention.

THINGS TO CONSIDER

Discussion Questions

1. Mr. Fields almost laughed at Dennis. How would the situation have changed if Mr. Fields laughed instead of becoming more irritated?
2. Mr. Fields had a lot on his mind when Dennis came in. Teachers will always have to juggle many issues at one time. How can a teacher begin to monitor his or her emotions and evaluate their effect on the students?
3. Had the other members of the class still been in the locker room would Dennis's behavior been different? Why or why not?
4. Based on what you have read, what do you think is Dennis's motivation for his behavior? Should a student's motivation be considered when disciplining a student for misconduct?
5. At the end of the scenario, Mr. Fields and Dennis are both angry. What are some other ways the situation could have been addressed to leave both parties in better frames of mind?

Areas for Reflection

The following concepts, theories, and strategies may offer some insight into the case study. It is worth exploring the effects these ideas would have on classroom management issues.

Characteristics of adolescents.   There are two major perspectives on an adolescent's life: the perspective of the adolescent and the perspective of his peers. During adolescence, the student is creating, re-creating, and evaluating his identity. Santrock (2003) talks about this process as self-understanding that is defined as "the adolescent's cognitive representation of the self, the substance and content of the adolescent's self-conceptions" (p. 292). During this period of time, the student is discovering who he or she is. The other factor in identity formation is the peer group. Santrock states that the peer group informs the adolescent about his or her ability as compared to other students the same age. Then the student can evaluate his or her performance and make adjustments in his or her self-concept. This time of discovery can lead to issues in the secondary classroom.

Rules and procedures.   Many classroom disruptions can be avoided by established classroom rules and procedures. Most classroom management texts agree that teachers should post three to five general rules for their classrooms (Canter & Garrison, 1994; MacDonald & Healy, 1999; Wong & Wong, 1998). These rules and procedures must be adapted for each teacher and classroom. For example, in the previous case study, Mr. Fields could not use the same rules and procedures as a senior-level English teacher. The procedures need to reflect the specific needs of the course. In this instance, how to dress, warm up, and clean up would be appropriate procedures. Rules may deal with sportsmanship, attitude, and horseplay. Good rules and procedures can help decrease if not eliminate many disruptions.

Using content as punishment.   Using content as punishment is not unique to physical education classes. English teachers and others have made students write sentences for years. Wong and Wong (1998) state that we should have logical consequences for misbehavior. They states that effective consequences "follow logically from the behavior rather than one that is arbitrarily imposed" (p. 155). If the violation is talking in class, a logical consequence may be relocating the student away from other peers, but not writing "I will not talk in class" 500 times. It is critical as teachers to promote a genuine, lasting interest in our content. English teachers want students to enjoy writing; PE teachers want students to develop a lifelong desire for fitness. By using the content as punishment, we are sending the message that the content is not fun, meaningful, or rewarding on its own. Rather, it is something unpleasant and painful.

ROLE-PLAY IDEAS

Case Study Cast: Mr. Fields, Dennis, and five to ten other students

1. Have students act out the complete scenario with dialogue. At the end, ask for suggestions for Mr. Fields to try with Dennis. What are some strategies he can use to reach Dennis now?
2. In small groups, have students brainstorm ways to prevent the situation or stop the situation from becoming as disruptive as it did. Have each group act out their best ideas and discuss them as a whole class.
3. Have students choose a motivation for Dennis (i.e., attention, peer acceptance). Based on the motivation, act out the ending of the scenario. Does the motivation make a difference in Dennis's behavior?
4. Have two to three students act out what the rest of the class would do after Dennis has left the gym. How has the incident affected the class?

7

GOSSIPING

At one time or another, everyone has been the subject of a rumor or gossip. In the secondary education classroom, rumors and gossip can be particularly damaging and destructive to an adolescent. Many students suffer ostracism from peers based on false accusations and stories. In the following case, we explore the power of rumors and gossips and their effects on students and classes.

THE SCENARIO

Mr. Landrum had been teaching eighth-grade Spanish for 18 years. He knew his content very well and he was able to draw on past experiences and lesson and still modify for today's students. For the past week, his classes have been working on cultural research on different Hispanic countries. He has set aside time today for each group to work on its presentation for the class. Students could choose to use the computers to do a Power Point project or use other resources in the class. This morning all of his classes had been on task and very productive.

Mr. Landrum was on his way back from the lounge. He went to check his mail and get a refill on coffee before third period started. As he walked along the hall, several students stopped to say hello and Ms. May, the social studies teacher, said good morning. Mr. Landrum thinks Ms. May seems to make it a point of speaking to him everyday. Maybe there is more to Ms. May than he thinks. All in all, Mr. Landrum was happy and confident on this fine spring morning.

The bell rang and class began as usual. Mr. Landrum took a moment to talk about events happening in the school and around town. The students were very excited about the upcoming Spring Carnival. Mr. Landrum asked if anyone would like to volunteer to work in the Spanish Club pie-throwing booth, and several students agreed. Then he transitioned to the lesson.

"Today you will have the rest of the class to work on your group presentations. I will be coming around to each group and checking on your progress. Please have questions ready for me. If you have a question before I get to your group, be patient; I will see everyone today," Mr. Landrum said.

Heath raised his hand. "Who has the computers today?" he asked.

"Well, we have five groups and three computers. I know Brazil and Mexico are using Power Point so they may each use a computer. Anyone else need a computer?" he asked.

Heath said his group, Guatemala, did. That left two groups working in the class with the other resources.

Mr. Landrum started with Brazil. They had a few questions, but were in pretty good shape. While they were conferencing, a roar of laughter went up from Colombia. Mr. Landrum offered the group a stern look and they settled down. What Mr. Landrum didn't see was Meg from the Cuba group turn bright red.

Mr. Landrum moved on to Mexico. Mexico was in worse shape than Brazil, so Mr. Landrum took some extra time with them to get them back on track. Meanwhile, over in Colombia, another round of laughter erupted. This time followed by angry voices. This time Mr. Landrum left Mexico to investigate the problems with Colombia.

"What is going on over here? I know it is not class work because Colombia is not that funny," Mr. Landrum said to the group.

"Oh, you know, Mr. Landrum, we are just having some girl talk," Rosa said. The rest of the group giggled.

"Well, quit it. Now is the time to work on Colombia, not your social lives," Mr. Landrum said as he wondered why he had allowed a group of all girls.

Mr. Landrum finished helping Mexico and went to consult with Guatemala. By far, Guatemala was ahead of the other groups. Mr. Landrum praised their hard work and began making his way to Cuba. A little burst of laughter came from Colombia, but a stern look quieted the girls down.

Mr. Landrum sat down with the Cuba group. Immediately, he noticed very little work was getting down, but no one seemed to be talking. "What have you all been doing over here?" Mr. Landrum asked as he looked around the group.

And then he saw Meg.

Meg, one of his nicest students, was sitting very still holding her arms around herself and quietly crying. Mr. Landrum was taken aback. In his 18 years of teaching, he had had girls cry in class before, but he would have never expected it from Meg. He wasn't prepared. "Meg, what's wrong?" Mr. Landrum asked.

"I don't know. I guess I don't feel well," Meg said.

At this point, Ben jumped in. "Mr. Landrum, one of those girls said something and showed a piece of paper and she came back crying."

Ben was pointing to the girls from Colombia.

Mr. Landrum had a bad feeling about this. He looked at Meg and then at the group of girls. "Meg, is what Ben said true?" he asked.

Mr. Landrum barely heard her muffled reply. "Yeah." He went over to the giggly bunch of girls led by Rosa.

"Where is the paper?" he asked.

"I don't know what you are talking about. We didn't do anything to Meg. She's just sensitive," Rosa said.

"Where is the paper?" he asked.

"Really, we don't have it," Rosa said.

"I am only going to ask once more. Where is the paper?" he asked.

Then he saw the crumpled sheet of paper being passed slyly from one student to the next. It had left Colombia, traveled through Brazil, and was working its way through Guatemala. Now everyone in the class knew what it said except Mr. Landrum.

Mr. Landrum intercepted the missive and read it. It said:

Hey Girl!
Guess what! I am *so* excited. You won't believe what happened! Yesterday, after school I was waiting for my mom and C.Z. was waiting for his mom. You know I have totally liked him for so long! Well, he *talked to me*!!! Can you believe it? I totally freaked! But he was all nice and it was okay. Do you think he likes me? I don't know what to do. I just kept thinking about kissing him all night. What should I do?
Write back,
Meg

As Mr. Landrum read the note, Meg began to cry harder. He looked at her in confusion and sympathy. And then Rosa opened her mouth.

"So now you know. Meg wants to kiss Chad. I bet she wants to have his babies, too. Chad won't ever kiss you. You are a stupid ugly cow. Besides, you are apparently a easy whore, too, if all you think about is kissing!" Rosa said.

Mr. Landrum turned quickly to Rosa. "Sit down and be quiet. I will deal with you in minute," he said. He then looked for Meg and couldn't find her. He heard the door slam and knew she had fled the scene.

Mr. Landrum knew middle school girls could be difficult, after all he had been teaching 18 years, but today was so far beyond anything he had ever seen in his class. He had never seen such unmitigated cruelty. And he did not know where to begin to repair the damage it had done.

BACKGROUND INFORMATION

The School

Mr. Landrum's school is a small school in a small town. Most of the faculty have been there five years or more. There is very little turnover. It is really a pleasant place to work. There is a larger town twenty miles away and some teachers commute to work. They like the smaller environment. The faculty and staff and students feel like a family. The most pressing problems the school faces are helping students from low-income homes and raising test scores. Over the years, there have been few fights or violent incidents. Overall, there is a welcoming feel to the school and the students and staff reflect a positive productive morale.

The Players

Mr. Landrum has been teaching 18 years with the past 15 of those years at his current school. Mr. Landrum met his wife at his previous school, and when they decided to move closer to her parents, they took jobs at this school. Mr. Landrum lost his wife in an automobile accident six years ago. Before her death, she was one of the most popular teachers on campus. Mr. Landrum and his wife were well liked by the staff and the students. After his wife's death, Mr. Landrum threw himself into his work. Over the past five years, Mr. Landrum has won Teacher of the Year for the school, district, and region. He has grown exponentially as a professional. It is just in the last year or so that Mr. Landrum has begun to emerge from his immersion in work. He has begun to socialize again and take an interest in other people and has started to mend ignored relationships. Finally, Mr. Landrum's professional and personal lives seem to be thriving.

Rosa is a Hispanic girl from a middle-class family. Her dad works as a supervisor at the local factory and her mother works as a nurse at the family care center. Rosa has two older brothers—one is in the Air Force and the other is a junior in high school hoping for a baseball scholarship to college. Rosa keeps an A/B average. Although it is mostly B's, she keeps an A in one or two classes to keep her parents off her back. Rosa is slim and tall for her age. She is really a stunning girl. All of these characteristics add up to Rosa being incredibly popular. All the boys want her attention, and the girls want to be her best friend. Rosa keeps a close group of girls around her most of the time. Her parents will not let her date, but that doesn't stop her from having a boyfriend at school, whom she changes every three weeks or so. All the students love Rosa, but the teachers see a little deeper. Many teachers have heard Rosa say mean things to the girls in her group and have watched her manipulate the boys to get their attention and favors. The teachers are at a loss; Rosa seems to have a strong and secure family background, but she obviously has a viscous mean streak for some reason.

Meg is a shy, smart girl. Meg is an only child in a lower middle-class family. Her father works shift work at the local factory and her mother works as a salesperson at the department store. When she is alone, Meg spends most of her time reading. She is very academic and not very athletic. She is introverted and withdrawn. At school, Meg has two close friends who have been her friends since elementary school. Meg is just developing as a woman and yet to lose her "baby fat." Teachers look at Meg and can see the beauty she will be in five years; students just see Mousy Meg. Meg is honest and sincere and teachers love her.

THINGS TO CONSIDER

Discussion Questions

1. Mr. Landrum used effective classroom management strategies such as eye contact, redirecting, and proximity control to manage the laughter from the group of girls. These techniques seemed to be working. How could Mr. Landrum have evaluated the situation more clearly? Were there signs that the behavior included more than off-task laughter?
2. Working in groups or with peers is an effective instructional strategy that also meets some of the social needs of the adolescent learner. What role did this instructional strategy have in the classroom disruption if any? Why or why not?
3. There were many instances in the case where Mr. Landrum could have avoided the final outcome. Where were these instances? What could he have done differently?
4. In this case, Mr. Landrum is not only dealing with inappropriate behaviors but also the emotional factors surrounding those behaviors. Should there be different approaches to each facet of the issue? If so, how would the strategies differ?
5. Mr. Landrum has three major people or groups to address: Meg, Rosa, and the class. All of these people need to be handled differently. Which person or group should Mr. Landrum handle first? Why?

6. Meg needs attention. She is crying and visibly upset. What options are available to Mr. Landrum to meet her needs? What are the benefits and drawbacks of each option?

Areas for reflection. The following concepts, theories, and strategies may offer some insight into the case study. It is worth exploring the effects these ideas would have on classroom management issues.

Peer groups. Most adolescents are members of a peer group. According to Santrock (2003), the groups can help with their self-esteem and identity formation. These groups like any other group have norms, or rules, for the members and roles, or positions, within the group. Santrock further states that students may also form cliques that are comprised of five to six individuals on average who are the same sex and age. Part of the clique functions are to "share ideas, hang out together, and often develop an in-group identity in which they believe their clique is better than other cliques" (Santrock, 2003, p. 204). Group and clique membership are normal behaviors for adolescents forming their identities and enhancing their self-esteem. However, these groups may affect the climate and tone of the secondary education classroom.

Respect. The idea of respect is critical in the secondary education classroom. You may hear teachers say "I demand respect from my students." However, respect in the classroom is a two-way street and cannot be demanded or ordered. In her book, *Authentic Classroom Management*, Barbara Larrivee (2005) states, "Respect is earned. You can gain it and you can lose it based on your deeds" (p. 80). Teachers cannot demand respect from students, just as students cannot demand respect from teachers or other students. However, teachers who treat students as individuals and valuable members of the class can establish a climate of respect among all class members as well as between teacher and student.

Modeling behaviors. Bandura (1986) states that humans learn more efficiently and effectively by observing and watching someone model the desired behavior. Modeling is an effective instructional strategy, but can also be a powerful tool in classroom management. Students who observe teachers behaving in a respectful and tolerant manner are more likely to mimic that behavior than those students who do not have a model to cue behavior. In some instances it may be more important for a teacher to take the time to model acceptance and forgiveness than it is for him or her to work one more math problem.

ROLE-PLAY IDEAS

Case Study Cast: Mr. Landrum, Rosa, Meg, and two to five other students

1. Have students act out the entire scenario with dialogue. Let the student playing Mr. Landrum try one or two strategies to discipline Rosa at the end. Discuss if they are effective.
2. Have one student portray Mr. Landrum and one student play Meg. Have students try two approaches to dealing with Meg. First, have the actors try talking in front of the class. Then have them talk in private. Discuss which approach is more effective.
3. Have students brainstorm ways to discipline Rosa in small groups. Have each group act out their best strategy.
4. Have a student portray Mr. Landrum as he addresses the entire class. What should he say? What would the reactions from the students be?

8

BLACK AND WHITE

The social dynamics of society play out in the classroom just as often as in other social institutions. The secondary education classroom has to address the same issues faced by the larger population of society including poverty, health care, hunger, and prejudice. The secondary education classroom can become a vehicle for social change if the teacher is prepared and tolerant. However, social issues can also cause disturbances. The following case deals with racial issues in a secondary education classroom.

THE SCENARIO

School had been in session for two weeks now and it was time for Mrs. Bradford to take her eleventh-grade chemistry class to the lab. Mrs. Bradford always likes taking the students to the lab. She knows that some students really can't grasp an idea until they actually try it out. Mrs. Bradford tries to incorporate as many labs into the school year as possible. Students get a hands-on activity plus an authentic learning experience. However, Mrs. Bradford dreads the day of picking lab partners. She is always worried that someone will be left out or not picked.

When Mrs. Bradford was in school, she was the one always picked last and she doesn't want any other child to feel the way she did when she was left behind. She has tried various ways to assign partners or randomly pair students over the years, but it seems that causes more trouble than it is worth. So, she lets students pick whom they want to work with and prays no one will get their feelings hurt.

On lab partner picking day, everything went pretty well. In first and second periods, Mrs. Bradford headed off having a left-over student by saying there could be one group of three and that worked well. As third period starts, Mrs. Bradford was relatively calm. This class had 28 students so there should be no student left over as they chose partners. Mrs. Bradford started class as usual with the science question of the day. As students wrestled with the question of ethics in pharmaceutical research, Mrs. Bradford took roll and finished her administrative chores. Mrs. Bradford enjoys third period. She has a diverse classroom comprised of 16 boys and 12 girls—four Hispanic students, nine black students, and 15 white students. Mrs. Bradford knows her community is not the most racially tolerant area in the state, and she tries valiantly to model tolerance and respect of the differences of her students. Today the students were discussing the question of the day in small groups and quieted down as Mrs. Bradford came to the front of the class.

"Good morning, class. Today we are going to pick our lab partners for the year. We have a big class and we have limited lab space, so we will be working in pairs for the duration of the class. I hope we will be able to work in the lab at least twice a month and hopefully more. So today you need to consider who you think you can work well with for that amount of time," Mrs. Bradford explained.

Katrina raised her hand. "So, we can pick anybody we want, right?"

"Yes, Katrina. You can pick anyone. However, once you have chosen your partner there will be no switching or changes; you will have to work with the person all year," Mrs. Bradford answered.

"All right, class. I am going to give you 10 minutes to find a partner. Once you have picked someone, please go to the lab and find an empty lab station to use," Mrs. Bradford instructed. "Are there any questions?"

No one raised a hand.

"Get to work," Mrs. Bradford said as looked at her watch. It was 10:35.

At 10:40, Mrs. Bradford noticed half the class had moved to the lab. Mrs. Bradford gave the students in the lab instructions on how to inventory their lab equipment. As they began to work, she returned to the classroom to motivate the stragglers.

"You have two minutes to find a partner and a lab station. Get busy," Mrs. Bradford said as she gathered some supplies from her desk. When she looked up, all the students were gone. Thank goodness, she thought. No problems with partners. And she made her way back to the lab.

When she got back to the lab, she surveyed all the lab stations. Everyone had a partner and was on task. Except Jason and Damon. Both boys were standing off to the side on opposite sides of the classroom. Jason was a white boy who stayed mostly to himself. When Mrs. Bradford asked him who his partner was he said he didn't have one. Damon was a popular black boy who was one of Mrs. Bradford's favorite students. When Mrs. Bradford asked Damon who his partner was he said everybody had a partner. Mrs. Bradford called the boys up to the front of the lab.

"Guys, I thought everyone had a partner. I am sorry I didn't catch it. You two are going to have to work together," Mrs. Bradford said. She knew that the boys knew each other. After all, it was a very small school and they had both been attending since kindergarten. Besides, Damon could work with anyone.

"Now, find a station. There is one open over there. And you can begin inventory on . . ." Mrs. Bradford did not get to finish her sentence.

"Hey, look. I am not going to work with him. I will just work by myself," Jason said.

"Jason, we don't have enough resources for you to work alone. You will work with Damon. Now get busy," Mrs. Bradford said.

"I will not work with that piece of crap. He's a nigger and he smells. You can't make me work with him!" Jason yelled.

All the color drained from Mrs. Bradford's face and Damon looked like he was going to be sick. Jason balled his fists in his hands and turned to Damon. Damon took a step toward Jason as Jason spoke.

"You are nothing. Just a worthless piece of crap. What kind of stupid black name is Damon anyway? You are good for nothing. My daddy says there ain't one thing niggers are good for," Jason spat.

Damon stopped moving and the class was silent. Mrs. Bradford could see Damon thinking through his options while his fist opened and closed. She had to do something fast.

Mrs. Bradford turned to Jason and spoke very slowly and quietly. "Jason, leave my classroom now."

Jason began to talk again, but Mrs. Bradford cut him off. "Jason, leave now."

Jason looked bewildered but began moving to the door mumbling that he didn't do anything wrong.

"Jason, get out and don't come back," Mrs. Bradford said.

And then he was gone.

Mrs. Bradford took a breath and turned to face the class. "If there is anyone else in this class that agrees with Jason, you may join him now," she began as she tried to salvage the class.

BACKGROUND INFORMATION

The School

Mrs. Bradford's school is a small rural school that is comprised of a majority of students from poor backgrounds. Despite the variety of ethnicities in the school, the school has struggled for years trying to integrate its facilities. Although there are all kinds of students, the students themselves tend to separate based on skin color and language. The school has tried various programs and strategies to get the students to interact. In the past year, nearly all of the fights on campus had been between students from different ethnic or language backgrounds. Instead of making progress in promoting tolerance and integration, the problems continue to get worse each year.

The Players

Mrs. Bradford is a veteran teacher with 20 years of experience. She was born and raised in the town and graduated from the same high school for which she currently teaches. She attended a regional state university and had no other dreams but to come back home and teach. And for twenty years, she has been happy. She married a new teacher her second year of teaching and they have two teenage sons. Mrs. Bradford was raised in a home where all people were celebrated, and she has raised her family that way as well. She is unsure how the racial tension has grown and seems to keep growing in the school. She is upset, but cannot think of what to do to solve the situation beyond what she does in her own classroom.

Damon comes from a family of five. His parents are married to each other and run a furniture store that is the family business. He has two sisters who are younger than he is. His family is very religious and active in the community. His father has been a powerful role model for Damon. Damon has lived a pretty sheltered life. His life has been filled with positive friends and family. He has never been the object of racial slur until today. He is a very good student and hopes to attend the Air Force Academy.

Jason lives with his parents and two older brothers. The family is very poor and both parents work. The older brothers both work at the refinery with their father; neither graduated from high school. Jason's mother is a positive influence in his life. She wanted to be a teacher, but got pregnant before she could go to college. She now works as a teacher's aide. Jason's father, however, is very bitter about the hand life dealt him. He sees everyone's success as a threat to his future. He holds no good feelings toward any fellow man. He is especially angry toward minorities. He feels his race is superior and he would be more successful if the minorities did not steal his promotions and jobs. He has ingrained his racial bigotry in his offspring.

THINGS TO CONSIDER

Discussion Questions

1. Given the scenario and the background information, what are some strategies, if any, Mrs. Bradford could have implemented to avoid a situation like this?
2. Mrs. Bradford essentially banishes Jason from the classroom. How effective is this solution? Are there better alternatives? If so, what?
3. Now that Jason has been removed from the classroom, Mrs. Bradford must address issues with Damon and the rest of the class. What are things she should do to reassure the class and Damon?

4. All students are shaped by their parents. Many will reflect the ideas and opinions of their parents for a lifetime while others mirror these ideas until they reach opinions of their own. How are we as educator supposed to challenge the thinking of students without denigrating the beliefs held by parents?

5. Some classroom issues are larger than that specific classroom. Racial tensions will cross over from class to class. What are some schoolwide strategies to address the need for tolerance and equality in a school?

Areas for Reflection

The following concepts, theories, and strategies may offer some insight into the case study. It is worth exploring the effects these ideas would have on classroom management issues.

Diversity. Previous chapters have included scenarios that depicted differences in ability and inclusive classrooms. However, students differ in more aspects than ability. Students differ in language, ethnicity, race, gender, socioeconomic status, religion, and sexual orientation as well as ability. These differences reflect the diverse population we now have in America. In an answer to the changes and multitude of differences in our students, educators have begun to focus on multicultural education. According to Sonia Nieto (2000), multicultural education can have an influence on most students' education. Nieto states that multicultural education can be a means to address student failure if implemented correctly. However, in addition to meeting the educational needs of all students we must also meet the social needs of those students. Schools must become a place to model tolerance and acceptance as well as appreciation of our differences.

Legal issues. Not only do teachers have a moral and ethical obligation to promote tolerance, but they also have a legal one. Fischer, Schimmel, and Stellman (2003) describe a violation of Title VI of the Civil Rights Act of 1964 in their book, *Teachers and the Law.* Parents of African American students sued the Tempe, Arizona, school district for violation of rights because their students were in classes that had a racially hostile environment. The students were subjected to name calling and derogatory graffiti while the administration made no effort to intercede. The courts ruled in favor of the parents and students (*Monteiro v. Tempe Union High*

School District, 2000). As we establish our classroom environments, it is critical to keep in mind the legal responsibilities we have as teachers.

Classroom structure.   The classroom structure can do a lot to prevent classroom disruptions. The Southern Poverty Law Center has a project called Teaching Tolerance (1999). This group published a manuscript titled "Responding to Hate at School: A Guide for Teachers, Counselors and Administrators," which includes many guidelines for creating a safe learning environment. Two major ideas are to provide support for victims and enforce appropriate consequences for offenders. The guidelines for supporting victims include:

- Confer with the victim's family;
- Use extreme sensitivity;
- Express regret;
- Encourage student outreach;
- Be sensitive to privacy concerns in anti-gay incidents. (pp. 29–30)

The guidelines for punishing offenders include:

- Involve the family of the offender;
- Involve a teacher whom the offender respects;
- Incorporate affirmative measures into "punishment";
- Strive to change biased attitudes;
- Seek student input. (pp. 31–32)

Many times teachers become too engrossed in rules about gum chewing and talking to realize the importance of guidelines or expectations about tolerant behaviors.

ROLE-PLAY IDEAS

Case Study Cast: Mrs. Bradford, Jason, Damon, and three to five other students

1. Have students act out the scenario with dialogue. At the end, let the student portraying Mrs. Bradford try different strategies to

comfort Damon and address the class. Students can then discuss which were most effective.

2. Have students brainstorm other ways Mrs. Bradford could have dealt with Jason after his immediate refusal to work with Damon. Then act them out. Were any effective in avoiding a racial incident?

3. Have two students portray Mrs. Bradford and Jason. What would their conversation be if she followed him out into the hall? Have different students try different approaches to talking with Jason. Which are effective?

4. Have students act out what would happen after Jason leaves. The student portraying Damon can improvise what he is thinking and feeling.

❾

AN ANGRY OUTBURST

Any combination of adolescent characteristics can lead to a possible classroom disruption. Adolescents are transitioning between childhood and adulthood and in that transition, they struggle with many issues. An authority figure in the classroom can be a source of discordance for a teenager. Students in secondary education classrooms are trying to assert their independence and autonomy and are still expected to follow rules and behave. In this case, a student is quick to anger over an issue with a teacher.

THE SCENARIO

Mr. McIver is a friendly and outgoing teacher, but lately he's begun to think he is letting his students get away with too much. He is a third-year teacher and when he compares his classroom to veteran teachers' classes, his seems too chaotic. So, after a little reflection, Mr. McIver decided he needed to instill more discipline and be meaner.

School had been in session for a week now. Mr. McIver was just now getting to the meat of the first unit in his English class. However, he had heard a great deal of whispering and seen some note passing and lots of off-task behavior. He has decided to revisit the class rules today and stop the misbehavior. The only problem Mr. McIver foresaw was that the students may not take him seriously after his friendly and lenient attitude last week, but he still thought he could make the change.

All of his classes went pretty well all day long. He did not expect anything different; most of his problems were in fifth period. The class is a mixture of average students and a few special education students and two honors students. His first unit of the year was on short stories. So far the class has read "The Scarlet Ibis" and the students were not very interested. Today they were going to get to choose they want to read and respond in journals. Mr. McIver thought that between giving them some options in the course and enforcing more rules the class would behave better and achieve more.

As the fifth-period bell rang, Mr. McIver was at the door to greet the students. Mr. McIver greeted students at the door everyday, but today instead of chatting and joking, he only nodded or grunted a welcome. As the students filed in, there was some discussion as to what was the matter with Mr. McIver. Some of the girls thought he was having a fight with his girlfriend while some of the boys maintained it was the poor performance of the football team that had Mr. McIver down. No matter what the hypothesis, everyone knew something was wrong with Mr. McIver.

As the students took their seats, Mr. McIver moved to the front of the class and began his well-prepared speech. "I know that we have only been in school for a week, but I feel that we are in dire need of a review of the rules and expectations of the class," he stated. Several students exchanged bewildered looks.

"As you are aware our class rules are posted on the bulletin board by the door," Mr. McIver said as he gestured toward the poster. The rules for his class are:

1. No talking.
2. Do your own work.
3. Raise your hand to speak.
4. Be respectful.
5. No horseplay.

As he gestured toward the poster, Mr. McIver realized that he has never enforced rule one or rule three and there actually has been no occasion to enforce the rest. In fact, if he is honest, he really isn't sure what he meant by rule four. He shook his head to clear his mind and got back to the speech.

"So from now on these rules will be enforced without exception. Am I clear?" Mr. McIver asked.

The students, looking slightly lost, nodded in agreement or looked out the window. But Mr. McIver seemed pleased as he switched to the day's lesson. If Mr. McIver had been paying as much attention to his class as his speech, he would have noticed that James had come into class with a scowl and was now mumbling under his breath rather heatedly, but Mr. McIver was already talking about the lesson.

"Since none of you seemed to be interested in "The Scarlet Ibis" I have decided to let you choose your own story to read today. I have several anthologies up here to choose from. Each student will pick a story and read it. Then you will write a three-page response to the story following the guidelines I will hand out later in class. Any questions?" Mr. McIver asked.

Juan began to speak. "Can't we . . ."

"Juan, you know you need to raise your hand before you talk," Mr. McIver said.

Juan chuckled and raised his hand.

"Yes, Juan?"

"Can't we work with a partner on this?" he asked.

"No, this is an individual assignment," Mr. McIver answered. He was pleased with himself for enforcing one of the rules. Then he heard some muttering.

"Rule one is no talking. Whoever is whispering needs to be quiet," Mr. McIver warned.

This time the muttering was louder and Mr. McIver could locate the source of the noise. James was in the back row apparently talking to himself. Mr. McIver walked a little nearer to James. Maybe his presence would silence the student. James, however, was in deep conversation with himself.

Mr. McIver could not make out many words, but he heard a few. ". . . can't believe . . . stupid pig . . . who does she think . . . I'm not . . . son of a . . ." were audible from James.

Mr. McIver did not need to hear any more. "Son of a . . ." was in violation of rules one and four. He knew this was a critical moment to prove to the class that he was serious about the rules and would enforce them without exception.

"James, you need to stop talking. You also need to watch what you say in this class. I will not have students using profanity. Consider this your warning," Mr. McIver said. Again, Mr. McIver was pleased with his performance as taskmaster.

James was not impressed nor was he pleased. "I didn't say anything profane. And I am not talking to anyone," James said.

"I heard you and I will not tolerate it," Mr. McIver answered. By this time, the exchange had the attention of the entire class.

"You are wrong." James stood up. Looking at his face, Mr. McIver could tell something went wrong. James was red-faced and on the verge of tears. "You are all alike. I thought you were different, Mr. McIver." James's voice grew louder with each word. "But I was wrong. You are as stupid and shallow and petty as all the rest of them. You are so quick to believe the worst of any student. Don't you have any feelings?"

And then James stopped talking and sat down and began to read a short story.

Mr. McIver looked around and gathered himself. He decided James didn't need any more discipline as he was on task so he returned to the front of the room to refocus the class on the lesson.

After class was over, Chloe stopped by Mr. McIver's desk. Chloe was a good student and sat in front of James.

"Mr. McIver, for what it's worth, James never did say any bad words. He was talking about his history teacher and he was upset about his grade. He said 'son of a gun.' I thought you might like to know," she said.

Mr. McIver was smart enough to know that he may have damaged his relationship with James beyond repair. How did he mess up so badly when he was trying to be so good?

BACKGROUND INFORMATION

The School

The school in which Mr. McIver teaches is a large ninth-grade center in a suburban area. The demographics of the school are typical of an urban area. There are many ethnicities, languages, religions, and socioeconomic levels represented in the school. The ninth-grade center was built to alleviate overcrowding in the high school, but in the few years since it opened the school has experienced tremendous growth. The facility can still accommodate the growing number of students, but the average class size has increased. Mr. McIver enjoys the atmosphere of the ninth-grade center and likes his current position.

The Players

Mr. McIver is a third-year teacher. He has been teaching at the ninth-grade center for the total of those years. In fact, his first year was the first year the center opened. He is slightly older for a new teacher. He tried working in the business world like his parents wanted him to do, but he was not happy. He has always known that he wanted to teach; it took a little maturing to be able to follow that desire. His family is a military family. His dad was career military in the Marines. Mr. McIver's desire to have a more casual and open classroom is probably a direct result of the confining and strict childhood he had. Mr. McIver has a good education in teaching and his content area. He also understands the dynamics of the community in which he works and lives. His major problem is classroom management. He wants to be friends with the students and have them like him and build relationships with them, but he also wants to avoid chaos and confusion. He has yet to resolve the two issues.

James is a typical adolescent. He is an average student from a good home. His parents are still married and both work for a national car company. James has one younger sister whom he likes. Although the family is by no means wealthy, they are comfortable. James's family attends the local Baptist church and he is active in the youth group. Overall, James is average, normal, and typical. The only variable that influences James's behavior is the fact he is an adolescent going through puberty.

THINGS TO CONSIDER

Discussion Questions

1. How did the classroom rules that Mr. McIver had posted contribute to his current situation? Were they effective or ineffective? Why?

2. Many new teachers feel that they need to be "mean" to students in the beginning. A better term may be strict. Is being a strict teacher more effective than not? Can a teacher have effective classroom management without being mean or strict?

3. In your opinion, can Mr. McIver make a change in the atmosphere of his classroom this far into the semester? Remember school has only been in session for a week, but he has come across as friendly and lenient during that time.

4. What are other responses that Mr. McIver could have made to James when James said he had not used profanity in order to prevent the situation from escalating?

5. At the end of the scenario, Mr. McIver discovers he is wrong. What are his options at this point? What would be the most effective response: to say nothing or admit he was mistaken? In your opinion, can he repair the damage to his relationship to James or not?

Areas for Reflection

The following concepts, theories, and strategies may offer some insight into the case study. It is worth exploring the effects these ideas would have on classroom management issues.

Fairness.   In *Scared or Prepared*, Canter and Garrison (1994) discuss the idea of fairness in connection to classroom management. First, they state, "if there is a climate of fairness in your classroom, you will have taken a large step toward the reduction of aggressive behavior" (p. 9). They hypothesize that students who feel they are being treated unfairly are more likely to act out aggressively or even violently in the classroom. In a later chapter they talk about using a clear well-developed discipline plan to establish fairness. According to these authors, a discipline plan should have clear rules that are simple and brief related to behaviors and a set of outlined consequences that are posted for the class to see. They also suggest that the class rules are enforceable at all times. Adolescents are not unique in their desire to be treated fairly; everyone wants to feel that the figure of authority is unbiased and consistent in judgments and punishments.

Communication.   In her book *Authentic Classroom Management*, Barbara Larrivee (2005) devotes an entire chapter to communication. Many times teachers communicate with students in such a way as to inhibit the conversation. Teachers talk down to students or demand specific behavior without discussion. Some teachers go so far as to use humiliation and sarcasm to change a student's behavior. Larrivee offers several suggestions for more open and positive communication with students. A few are:

- Encourage rather than praise.
- Use nonjudgmental responses.
- Use "I" statements. "I need you to . . ."
- Develop listening skills.

As teachers it is important to listen to ourselves speak to students. It is easy to fall into a communication pattern that only offers a one-way dialogue.

Character education.   Character education has picked up momentum in the public schools in past years. Santrock (2003) defines character education as "a direct approach that involves teaching students a basic moral literacy to prevent them from engaging in immoral behavior and doing harm to themselves or others" (p. 394). In today's society, teachers are not only expected to teach their content's curriculum but also act as moral exemplar for students. There are times when a class disruption can become a teaching moment for character education. Again it is imperative for teachers to model the very behaviors they expect from their students.

ROLE-PLAY IDEAS

Case Study Cast: Mr. McIver, James, Chloe, and two to five other students

1. Have the students act out the scenario with dialogue. Let students make suggestions for strategies to try to address the problem with

James. Have students act out several suggestions and discuss which were most effective.

2. In small groups, have students brainstorm ways to approach James in the next class. Have each group act out their solution. The whole class can discuss which were most effective and why.

3. Have two students act out what James would say to his best friend after class. Let students discuss why this perspective is important.

MS. POPULARITY

Out of school there is no equal to the powerful phenomenon of popularity. The students who are considered popular in school hold a special status in the eyes of their peers and sometimes even their teachers. The popular students are sometimes afforded special treatment that the average students are not. At times the special treatment, in addition to the attention from peers, sends the message to the popular student that he or she is in fact different from everyone else. Teachers must be careful not to be biased toward any student. In this case, the student tries to use her leverage as a popular student, and the teacher must deal with unwanted advances.

THE SCENARIO

Mr. Cobb has been teaching civics/economics at this urban high school for ten years. He has a genuine passion for government and civics and enjoys interacting with the upperclassmen. He teaches four sections of civics/economics and one section of history. He has been happy with his classes this year. The students have been attentive and there have been few disruptions. Mr. Cobb feels lucky to be teaching in the school district he is in; it is financially stable and has little violence or crime. Some of Mr. Cobb's friends work in districts where the teachers' main concern is for their own safety rather than the education of their students.

For the past three weeks, the students in Mr. Cobb's civics/economics class had been studying the stock market. Each student was "given" $2,500 to invest in stocks. Everyday the students check the stock market report and track the progress of their stocks. After three weeks, the students were to write a paper reviewing the performance of their stocks and forecast the next three weeks for each stock they have invested in. For fun, the student that has amassed the most gain in six weeks will win a small prize. However, Mr. Cobb thinks everyone will come away with a better understanding of the market and investing. Today marked the end of the three-week period. Each student should have a report ready to hand in and discuss concerning his or her investment portfolio.

The bell rang for fourth period and the students ambled in. Fourth period is after lunch and there are always a few stragglers. Mr. Cobb usually waits three minutes after the tardy bell for latecomers; today was no different. The students are aware of Mr. Cobb's policy and try hard to make it to class on time; they know Mr. Cobb doesn't have to give them extra time and they appreciate the gesture.

As the class settled down, Mr. Cobb began the lesson. "Today we need to hear everyone's report on the progress of their stocks. Let's just go down the row. Everyone will have two minutes to brief us on his or her progress. Let's start with Erin," Mr. Cobb said.

Erin stood up and began to talk about her investments. She had split her money into three separate stocks and was ahead in each of them. Joe went next and talked about his investment in an energy company that was losing money, and, unfortunately, he had put all his eggs in one basket. During Joe's report, Jessica slipped through the door and found her seat two chairs behind Joe.

Next, Anthony reported on the 12 different stocks for which he divided his $2,500. Brittany, who sat in front of Jessica, was getting ready to give her report when Jessica tapped her shoulder.

"Hey, what are we doing?" Jessica asked.

"You have to give your report on your stocks. You are next after me," Brittany whispered back before she stood up.

While Brittany talked about diversification of investments, Jessica wracked her brain to recall any sort of report she was supposed to prepare. To make matters worse, she had not checked on the status of her stocks for four days. She had no idea if she was ahead or behind at the moment. As Brittany sat down, Jessica had no idea what she was going to do.

After waiting a moment for Jessica to stand and start talking, Mr. Cobb spoke. "Jessica, it's your turn."

"What? Oh, Patrick can go ahead of me. I'll be ready in a minute," Jessica replied with a bright smile. Jessica was used to getting her way. She was head cheerleader and hands down the most popular girl on campus. On top of that, she was tall, slender, blue-eyed, and blonde. She was not accustomed to people telling her "no."

"Well, Jessica, that is very nice of you, but it is your turn and if you don't give your report now, you will receive a zero on the oral portion," Mr. Cobb said.

"But, Mr. Cobb, I am not quite ready. I was late and I need to get my things together. I will just take a minute. Patrick, go ahead," Jessica said.

Patrick, blinded by the reflection off Jessica's white teeth, started to stand.

"Patrick, please take your seat. Jessica, this is the last time I will ask you to give your report before I record a zero. Are you ready?" Mr. Cobb said.

Jessica stood up. "Mr. Cobb, could I talk to you a moment in private?" Jessica asked as she looked down demurely.

"Fine. Come up to my desk." Mr. Cobb was a little irritated. He hated interruptions in his class, but he also wanted to give students the benefit of the doubt, which is why he allowed Jessica a private conference. "Class, give me a minute with Jessica and then we will proceed."

Jessica walked up to Mr. Cobb's desk and smiled to herself. She knew if she could talk to him alone, she could make him see it her way. At his desk, Jessica leaned over so she could look into his eyes.

Mr. Cobb was not in the mood for wasting time. "Jessica, what is it?" he asked.

"Mr. Cobb, to tell you the truth, I don't have my report." As Mr. Cobb sighed, Jessica pressed on. "I have been so busy. You know, homecoming is next week and I am swamped with the pep rally and bonfire and dance preparations. And, on top of that, my dog, Sugar, is sick and I have to take care of her at night." At this point, Jessica managed to force a single tear to fall from the corner of her eye down her cheek. "Could you please let me have one more day? I will have my report for you first thing in the morning," Jessica said as she put her hand on Mr. Cobb's hand.

As Mr. Cobb considered his responses, Jessica leaned in and pretended to straighten his tie while touching his chest. At her slight touch, Mr. Cobb was spurred to action. Not unaware of the entire classroom's attention, Mr. Cobb stood up.

"Jessica, return to your seat. You have one minute to produce your report or you will receive a zero," Mr. Cobb stammered.

Jessica took a minute to look at him and straighten her short skirt before she answered. "Are you sure, Mr. Cobb?"

BACKGROUND INFORMATION

The School

Mr. Cobb teaches in a very affluent high school in a suburban area. Although the school building is over 20 years old, it is clean and well maintained. The surrounding community is stable and solid. The growth of the high school has reached a plateau in the past few years. The surrounding neighborhoods are safe and friendly, and the turnover in homeowners is low. The majority of the families are upper middle class and professional. There are a wide variety of ethnic and religious groups in the area, but all groups support the school and the students.

The Players

Upon graduation from high school, Mr. Cobb married his sweetheart and joined the Marines. He enjoyed his time in the service and the different locations he was stationed. Unfortunately, his wife enjoyed Marines, too; she had an affair with another serviceman. Their marriage ended after three years and Mr. Cobb finished his enlistment and was honorably discharged. Mr. Cobb had always had a desire to teach, and, after serving his country, he was ready to serve its youth. He finished a certification program along with a history degree and found his first job. He had a new life and career. After a decade of teaching, Mr. Cobb is still happy with his choice. He has found a place he belongs. For the past two years, he has been dating the family and consumer science teacher and will be proposing soon.

Jessica comes from a very wealthy family. Her father is an internationally known corporate lawyer who on average spends two days home a month. Her mother mostly spends her days at the country club or at one of her charity events. Jessica sees very little of her parents and spends her time on high school social events. She dictates the social scene at the high school. Jessica sees her mother enough to stay annoyed with her, but she truly misses her father. She envies her friends who have fathers who participate in their lives. Even though Jessica enjoys the comfort of her affluent life, she longs for a normal family and doting parents.

THINGS TO CONSIDER

Discussion Questions

1. What should be Mr. Cobb's primary concern at the end of the scenario? What are his options for a response?
2. Obviously, Jessica is using sexual advances to manipulate a situation for her advantage. There is a difference between her behavior and an innocent crush on a teacher. How can situations like the one with Jessica be avoided? Should teachers treat students like Jessica differently from students with crushes?
3. Given Mr. Cobb's classroom policies, are there any changes or strategies that could be implemented to avoid the confrontation with Jessica? In other words, did Mr. Cobb's tardy policy help or hinder the situation?
4. Was a one-on-one conference an appropriate solution to the situation? Why or why not? What are some alternatives?

5. Jessica felt she had the power to control the situation based on her status in the school. Do teachers feed into the student social hierarchy or not?

Areas for Reflection

The following concepts, theories, and strategies may offer some insight into the case study. It is worth exploring the effects these ideas would have on classroom management issues.

Classroom procedures. Having clear concise procedures and rules in your classroom can cut down on possible disruptive incidents. Wong and Wong (1998) offer a few suggestions for starting class. First, make sure students know what is expected of them at the beginning of class. They suggest a bell activity that will engage the students in content-related work as soon as they enter the room. Everyday students know what is expected and where to find the instructions and materials. Second, they state to use logical consequences. In one of their examples, an illogical consequence for tardiness is the teacher ignoring the behavior while a logical consequence is the student "misses instruction and suffers the consequences" (p. 155). In addition, it may be beneficial to have written rules and consequences, as opposed to Mr. Cobb's unwritten policy on lateness.

Popularity. Santrock (2003) discusses membership in crowds that is based on reputation where the members may or may not spend time together. The crowds may break down into smaller groups called cliques. Santrock says that groups are usually defined by the activities the members participate in or the social interactions of the groups. Examples of these groups include jocks, popular students, normals, druggies, and nobodies (Brown & Lohr, 1987). The jocks and the popular students are at the top of the social hierarchy, while the nobodies are at the bottom. Obviously, there is a structured social hierarchy in secondary education classrooms. Although teachers need not reinforce the social stratification, it is helpful and insightful for teachers to understand where a certain student sees him- or herself fitting in and where his or her peers see that person fitting. Not everyone can be popular. However, the pressure to fit in can be enormous for an adolescent. In addition, the social conventions of adolescents may afford popular students special status and deny members of the groups held in lower regard social opportunities.

Sexuality.   Each generation in America has had to cope with issues of sexuality in its own way. The 1960s launched the sexual revolution, while the 1980s emphasized safe sex with the rampant spread of AIDS. Today's adolescent is bombarded with messages regarding sex and sexual attraction. Advertising is filled with sexual promotions, and many television shows depict sexual behavior or discuss sexual activities. Within this environment of marketed sexuality the adolescent must develop his or her own sexual identity. Santrock (2003) states that the adolescent must learn how to deal with sexual feelings and manage intimacy issues, along with developing physically, socially, and cognitively. As teachers, we need to be aware of the struggles the adolescent is going through besides cognitively and academically. The sexual development of an adolescent can cause issues in his or her life just as any other area of development.

ROLE-PLAY IDEAS

Case Study Cast: Mr. Cobb, Jessica, and two to five other students

1. Have students act out the scenario with dialogue. Let the student portraying Mr. Cobb try different responses to Jessica's final question. The whole class can discuss which responses are most effective.
2. In small groups have students brainstorm alternative ways Mr. Cobb could have dealt with Jessica without giving her an opportunity to speak with him in private. Each group can act out its best solution.
3. Have two students act out a conversation between Jessica and a close friend. Jessica can show insights into what she was thinking during class and her conversation with Mr. Cobb.

III

CLASSROOM MANAGEMENT AND SPECIAL CIRCUMSTANCES

Although teachers have a large amount of control and influence on the majority of factors that contribute to successful or ineffective classroom management, there are also a few situations that are out of the control of the teachers. Teachers can plan effective instruction and practice classroom management strategies and still find themselves in a situation that they have not anticipated. The final section of the book includes case studies that address special circumstances that can occur in a classroom. By no means should any teacher expect all of these scenarios to happen in his or her career, but everyone should think about possible ways to prevent these situations and what they would do if they should occur.

Schools are microcosms of larger society and as such are comprised of the same attributes of the macrocosm. Just as there are violence and hostilities in the real world, there is violence in schools. Secondary school teachers have long been familiar with fights on campus. It seems that fights have been a characteristic of the high school and middle school campus for some time. Although fighting may be common in schools, it is not an everyday occurrence, yet it is still a serious issue for students, teachers, administrators, and parents. In addition, the media have focused on extreme violence in schools over the past decade.

There have been extreme violent incidents in the schools like Jonesboro and Columbine that have changed the way schools function. Before those violent attacks, it was uncommon to see a metal detector at a school entryway; today it is not so rare. Schools have also included police officers as part of the staffing pattern. Again, the odds are that a teacher will not have to contend with an armed student in his or her career, but it is foolhardy and overly optimistic to not consider preventative measures and strategies to handle such an encounter. One other circumstance that can disrupt a classroom is a confrontation with a parent. Most classroom management strategies are focused on managing the misbehavior of the students, but it is equally important to consider how to protect your class when an outside factor disrupts the learning environment. As stated previously, these situations are unique and infrequent, but the effective classroom manager will consider all the possibilities for disruption.

Overall, the classroom teacher has a great deal to prepare and deliver in his or her classroom. Teachers create objectives, lectures, activities, assessments, and more while considering the best ways to implement those with the least amount of disruption and confusion. On top of the day-to-day planning and delivery, the effective classroom manager also constantly assesses the possibilities of violence and danger in the classroom. In today's schools, it is better to be overly prepared than to ignore the possibilities of an extreme violent incident occurring in the classroom.

11

A POWER STRUGGLE

One of the major dangers in any class is a power struggle with a student. A power struggle usually consists of a teacher issuing demands to a student and that student refusing to comply. The more the teacher demands, the more resistant the student becomes. This type of encounter can change the atmosphere of a classroom for the rest of the year. A teacher can lose all credibility and authority in a matter of minutes in a power struggle; or, if handled effectively, reinforce the classroom expectations and desired behaviors. The following scenario depicts a power struggle between a teacher and a student.

THE SCENARIO

Mrs. Taylor teaches tenth-grade geography. She has been teaching English for the past five years. This year, she has been assigned geography and history due to No Child Left Behind (NCLB) requirements. When she was hired to teach, the school needed an English teacher, and, although she was not certified in English, she did have a minor and there were no other viable applicants. Now, thanks to NCLB, all teachers must be certified in the content area they are teaching, so the district moved her to geography and history. After teaching English, she realized she enjoyed the content more than history and is now slightly upset and disappointed about the change of teaching assignment.

Even though it is midterm, Mrs. Taylor still has not adjusted to her new content area. When she taught English, she was excited and inspired; now with her geography class, all she can come up with for instruction are maps and worksheets. She doesn't seem to have the passion for teaching she had when she was teaching English. She just doesn't care about geography. In fact, Mrs. Taylor is so disheartened that she is thinking of leaving teaching altogether.

It was the week before midterm exams and Mrs. Taylor planned for her classes to finish the maps of Africa today so that they can move on to a review tomorrow. Students had been working individually on a book of maps of the countries in Africa. Each student must choose ten countries to map and characterize for his or her book. They have had two weeks to work on it in class and today was the final day. Mrs. Taylor hoped to just make it through the next week and to regroup over the holidays.

As students for first period wandered in, Mrs. Taylor set out the geography books and finished her coffee. The students found their seats and started pulling out their work and supplies.

"Good morning. I hope you are all doing well this morning. We have a lot of work to do. Today is the last day to work on your map books. You have the whole class period to finish up any map and we will hand them in at the end of the period. Remember, this is not a group project. Do you own work and no talking," Mrs. Taylor said.

Mrs. Taylor felt she had given ample instructions and returned to her desk to finish entering the attendance and then get online to read today's news. The students had been working on their own for two weeks and Mrs. Taylor knew they were all right. She figured most of them were finished anyway; the stragglers would finish today and they could move on. To her credit, Mrs. Taylor did take a look around the room every few minutes to make sure the students were on task.

As she looked up to check on the class, Mrs. Taylor noticed Michael was not in his seat. Michael was somewhat of a cut-up. He was very social and thought of himself as very entertaining. He was not one of Mrs. Taylor's favorite students, and today she was in no mood to deal with him.

"Michael, get back to your seat," Mrs. Taylor said.

"Hey, Mrs. Taylor, I am only trying to borrow some map colors. I lost mine," Michael explained.

"I don't care why you are out of your seat. Return to it now," Mrs. Taylor said.

Michael returned to his seat slowly. He sat down and watched Mrs. Taylor. As soon as she was busy reading the headlines on the Internet, he got up and went back to Julia's desk. He just needed three map colors to finish his last map and his project would be done.

As Michael was charming the map colors away from Julia, Mrs. Taylor looked up for a check of the class. Needless to say, she was not happy to see Michael out of his seat again.

"Michael, I have already told you to return to your seat. Now sit down and stay there," Mrs. Taylor said.

"Give me one second. I need to get these map colors from Julia," Michael said.

"Sit down now," Mrs. Taylor said.

"Fine," Michael said as he marched back to his seat. "Can I borrow a map color from you, Mrs. Taylor?"

Mrs. Taylor had had enough from Michael today. "No, if you are not prepared to do your work, you will have to face the consequences and receive a low grade," Mrs. Taylor informed him.

This news did nothing to make Michael feel any better or want to stay in his seat. As soon as Mrs. Taylor was busy again, Michael returned to Julia's desk.

And Mrs. Taylor saw him.

"Michael! Get in your seat right now. I do not want to see you out of it until the final bell rings! Do you understand me?" Mrs. Taylor all but yelled.

"Look, I am just getting the map colors," Michael explained.

"I don't care. Sit down!" Mrs. Taylor said.

"I am not sitting down without map colors. I want to finish my work!" Michael said.

And that was the last straw.

"YOU will sit down now," Mrs. Taylor yelled.

"No! You are being unfair. I will not sit down until I get some map colors!" Michael yelled back.

By this time, Mrs. Taylor was on her feet and headed toward Michael. As she approached, she held out her hand to grab his arm. "Michael, sit down," she said.

"Don't touch me! I didn't do anything wrong. You are just picking on me!" Michael yelled.

"Michael, this is the last time I am going to ask you, sit down," Mrs. Taylor said.

"What are you going to do? Make me? You can't make me do anything! This is so stupid!" Michael said. And with that he kicked over his desk and knocked things off the shelves on his way out of the classroom. Then he slammed the door.

Mrs. Taylor was a turmoil of emotion. She was glad he was gone. She was still angry with him, but she was also confused as to how things got so heated so fast. And she was embarrassed to have lost control of the class. She looked around the room and all the students were watching her to see what she would do next.

Slowly, she bent down to right the desk, stalling for time for what to say.

BACKGROUND INFORMATION

The School

Mrs. Taylor works at a small rural school. The school serves a population of 1,000 high school students. The school has had to do some restructuring due to the NCLB mandates made by the federal government. Historically, it has been difficult to find qualified teachers to fill vacancies in the district. Most of the teachers are individuals who want to be in the area because it is their hometown or their hometown is close. Therefore, the administration has made a practice of hiring people who are certified and want to teach in their own school and placing them in whatever vacancy is open at the time regardless of teaching field. Now, with NCLB, and the mandate that all teachers must be certified in their teaching field, the school has had to reassign teachers and even cut some programs for which there are no certified teachers, like theater. The school has made some dramatic changes, but has hopes for a better school and learning environment in the end.

The Players

Mrs. Taylor has been an English teacher for five years at this high school. She is typical of the type of teacher the district hires. Mrs. Taylor grew up in the area and wanted to return to be close to family. When she applied there were no openings for a history teacher and there were no other applicants for the English position, so she was hired as an English teacher. During her first year, she discovered that she loved teaching English and could never really imagine going into a history class. Now with her change in assignment, Mrs. Taylor is wondering about her options. She could pick up more courses and get certified in English, but she didn't really enjoy school. During the time she is getting certified, she would have to teach history. The more she has thought about it, the more she thinks she would like to get out of teaching. The students seem to be more and more irresponsible and impolite. She is running out of patience. Mrs. Taylor is married and her husband works as a mechanic. He owns his own shop. There is the possibility she could work with him. On the other hand, she wants to have a baby and teaching allows for a great schedule for working moms. She is torn about what to do. She really doesn't enjoy teaching anymore, but what else can she do?

Michael lives with his mom and stepfather. His mom cleans houses and his stepfather is a postman. His mother and father divorced when Michael was a toddler and he has had no contact with his father since. Michael's mother has been married to his stepfather for eight years since Michael was seven. His family is not very well off, but they pay their bills on time and manage to save a little. Michael has always been his mother's joy. When she and Michael were struggling on their own, Michael always cheered her up with jokes and impressions. Michael's mother adores the fact that her son is funny. He has rescued her from tears on many occasions. Michael is encouraged by his mother and hopes to go to college to major in drama.

THINGS TO CONSIDER

Discussion Questions

1. How did Mrs. Taylor's attitude toward her content area and class contribute to the confrontation?
2. At times a teacher's emotions, like any other person, will get the best of him or her. How can teachers monitor and adjust to keep their emotions in balance to avoid a classroom disruption?
3. There were several times that Mrs. Taylor could have changed the course of the confrontation. What were they and what could she have done differently?
4. In every power struggle there comes a point when neither side can back down without losing face. For the teacher, backing down could mean losing some authority in the classroom. At what point did the confrontation become a lose-lose situation for Mrs. Taylor and Michael?
5. What are some logical consequences for Michael's lack of preparedness? What are things you can do in your classroom to maintain learning despite the lack of student preparation?

Areas for Reflection

The following concepts, theories, and strategies may offer some insight into the case study. It is worth exploring the effects these ideas would have on classroom management issues.

Consequences.   The consequences students face based on their behavior are key to changing that behavior. Too often teachers spend the majority of their time constructing rules and procedures with fleeting or no attention to the consequences to be enforced for such behaviors. Larrivee (2005) offers three types of consequences: natural, logical, and arbitrary. Natural consequences occur inevitably from a specific behavior. For example, if you stick your hand in a fire, it will get burned. It happens automatically. In a classroom a natural consequence of talking is not hearing instruction. The next type of consequence is logical. As discussed in earlier chapters, a logical consequence is designed by a teacher to relate directly to the behavior. A student writing on a desk is made to clean the desks. Arbitrary consequences are enforced by the teacher but do not relate to the behavior in question. An example is a late student made to write 500 sentences stating he will not be late again, compared to the natural consequence of missing instruction or a logical consequence of making up the time after class. An effective classroom management plan includes logical consequences that help redirect student behaviors; ineffective classroom managers offer arbitrary or no consequences for behavior.

Strategies. Most classroom management texts will offer strategies to use in different situations. In *Classroom Management for Middle and High School Teachers* (Emmer, Everston, & Worsham, 2006), the authors offer strategies for minor and moderate disruptions and then extensive interventions for more serious incidents. For minor disruptions the authors suggest:

- Use nonverbal cues;
- Get the activity moving;
- Use proximity;
- Redirect the behavior;
- Provide needed instruction;
- Issue a brief desist;
- Give the student a choice;
- Use an "I-message." (pp. 174–175)

For moderate disruptions the authors provide strategies that include:

- Withhold a privilege or desired activity;
- Isolate or remove students;
- Use a fine or penalty;
- Assign detention;
- Use school-based consequences. (pp. 176–178)

Finally, for more serious offenses, the authors include other interventions:

- Design an individual contract with the student;
- Hold a conference with a parent;

- Use a check or demerit system;
- Use problem solving;
- Use the "think time" strategy;
- Use peer mediation. (pp. 170–186)

Classroom teachers need to be familiar with different strategies to manage their classes. As one becomes more confident and competent using various strategies, the application will become second nature.

Power.   As with any human being, students desire power or a sense of control over situations in their lives. A student who wants power in a classroom can cause major disruptions in that class. Charles H. Wolfgang (2001) characterizes those students:

> A student who wishes to possess power should not be able to engage the teacher in a struggle. The teacher who falls for this "bait" and gets pulled into the battle is merely continuing the excitement and challenge for the student. The student becomes increasingly bolder and pleased with trying to test the teacher. The teacher should attempt to remove the issue of power altogether and force the student to look for some other goal for behaving. (p.121)

In any given classroom, there may be many students who are willing to engage in a power struggle with a teacher. A student in one class may push the teacher everyday while behaving beautifully for the teacher in the next classroom, which makes it imperative for teachers to invest the time to know students on an individual level. The more a teacher connects with and takes genuine interest in her students, the less likely a major disruption is to occur.

ROLE-PLAY IDEAS

Case Study Cast: Mrs. Taylor, Michael, Julia, and two to five other students

1. Have students act out the entire scenario with dialogue. Afterward, have students discuss how Mrs. Taylor was feeling during the incident and how Michael was feeling.

2. Have students act out various strategies for Mrs. Taylor to implement with the class after Michael leaves. Discuss which are more effective.

3. In small groups, have students brainstorm ways that Mrs. Taylor could have avoided the confrontation. Have each group act out one strategy and discuss which would be most effective.

4. Have two students act out what could possibly happen between Mrs. Taylor and Michael on the next day. Discuss what needs to be done to help Michael.

⓬

VIOLENT STUDENTS

One of the most serious and dangerous classroom disruptions is a violent confrontation between students. Many teachers proceed through their entire career without witnessing or managing a fight, while others are not as fortunate. Many principals and teachers would probably say that most violent confrontations between students happen before or after school, between classes, or at lunch. However, it is possible for students to start a fight in the middle of a class. The following scenario describes a violent confrontation between two students in a history class.

THE SCENARIO

Mrs. Ogden was glad it was the last class period of the day. Not only was it the last class of the day, it was the last class of the week. The day had been crazy. It was a game day and there were announcements and assemblies and a bunch of other nonsense. Mrs. Ogden could not see the reasons for such goings on. The preparations for a Friday night high school football game seemed completely out of hand to her. Besides, all that hoopla only agitated the students and made them more unruly than they already were.

Normally, Mrs. Ogden ran a very structured class with little disruption. She is very mild mannered and soft spoken. Mrs. Ogden has been teaching for over 20 years. She has infinite knowledge of her content area and continues to pursue varied professional development opportunities each year. After struggling for a few years as a new teacher, Mrs. Ogden began to understand her classes and found her own style of classroom management, which has remained effective all these years. Her class is very orderly with clear expectations and consequences. Each year she may have one or two students challenge her at the beginning of the year, but after those are dealt with the class settles down and begins to work on history. Over the years, she has had few serious classroom disruptions and she feels comfortable and confident in her classroom management and instructional abilities.

Today, however, Mrs. Ogden is slightly agitated. She has been taking care of her mother for the past six months. Her mother has Alzheimer's disease and needs care. She has been living with Mrs. Ogden for the past few months and things were going well; however, Mrs. Ogden has realized she now needs around the clock care. The interview at the nursing home is scheduled for 4:30 today. Mrs. Ogden is dealing with the stress of caring for her mother alone. And, to top it off, school had been quite trying this week with the big game and many other interruptions. Mrs. Ogden can't seem to focus nor can she get her students focused for very long. So today she was letting the students finish their group work to prepare for presentations next week. She hoped they will work and when they finish they can have free time. Only one more class to go.

Seventh period started like all the other classes. The students came in and chattered and gossiped. They were very excited about the game with their long-time rival tonight. In seventh period, Mrs. Ogden has two cheerleaders, three football players, four band members, and many devoted fans. All all of which leads to much chaos, making it a challenge to start class. Eventually, Mrs. Ogden got everyone seated and commands the students' attention.

"Good afternoon. I know you are all very excited about tonight as am I," Mrs. Ogden started. "But we do have important work to finish in class today. I want you to work in your small groups on your presentations for next week. We will begin presenting on Monday. The order is posted on the board. If you finish before the bell, you may sit quietly and work on something else. If you do not finish before the bell, you must finish it this weekend. Any questions?" Mrs. Ogden asked.

No one raised a hand.

"Okay. Please begin working," Mrs. Ogden said.

The students grouped up and began working. Mrs. Ogden could hear talk in the groups about the football game and the dance, but the room was relatively quiet and the students were working while they were talking, so Mrs. Ogden did not say anything. Instead, she moved from group to group to check on each group's progress. All groups were on track and she thought everyone would finish before the class ended. Mrs. Ogden breathed a sigh of relief and sat at her desk to finish her lesson plans for next week.

Over on the side of the class by the windows, two boys were talking about the football game. Steven, a junior, was on the football team and Brad, also a junior, was a notoriously popular bad boy.

"I think we are really gonna kick some butt tonight," Steven said.

"Yeah? Well, we'll see," replied Brad.

"Have you been following the other team? I mean they are 2-4 for the season and I heard their quarterback hurt his little finger," Steven said laughing. "No way are they gonna take us!"

"If you are so sure, why don't you put your money where your mouth is?" Brad asked.

"What do you mean?" Steven asked.

"Just a friendly little wager. I'll bet you $50 that you get beat tonight," Brad asked.

"Hey, you know, betting is wrong. I can't do that," Steven said.

"Ohh. So you aren't so sure you're gonna win. Too scared to take a teeny tiny bet," Brad taunted.

"Hey! I am not scared. I think betting is wrong. Everyone knows that. And we are going to win tonight," Steven said.

By now Mrs. Ogden had noticed the intense conversation, although she was not sure what they were talking about. "Boys, quiet down and get back to work," Mrs. Ogden said.

The boys started to work again, but Brad thought Steven was too easy a mark to stop teasing. "Hey, Steven, I know what it is—you just talk big 'cause you're so scared to go play football. You're just hoping you don't have to play 'cause you don't want to get tackled. You are such a little girl!" Brad said.

In the blink of an eye both boys were standing up nose to nose and the rest of the class was watching with open mouths.

"Take it back, Brad. I am no sissy. You were too scared to even try out for the team," Steven said through clenched teeth.

"No way. You are a pansy. Pansy! Pansy! Pansy!" Brad yelled.

And in that moment Steven was no pansy. From the punch he threw at Brad, you would have thought he was John Wayne. And the fight was on.

As desks were knocked over, Mrs. Ogden ran to the back of the classroom yelling the whole way. "Boys! Boys! Stop at once. Stop it!"

The boys continued to scuffle for about thirty more seconds and then as they each tired, they each allowed a friend to pull them out of the fray. Mrs. Ogden was furious and scared.

"I told you to stop. I told you to do your work. What is wrong with you? What would possess you to fight in class?" Mrs. Ogden demanded.

The boys speaking at once began blaming the other immediately. Mrs. Ogden told them to be quiet and led them out of the class by the arm to the office. As she left the classroom with the two boys, she turned to survey the class one last time. Desks were overturned; papers and books were scattered. Students stood around laughing and recounting the entire incident. What had happened? She had no idea.

What a great way to end the week.

BACKGROUND INFORMATION

The School

This school is a suburban high school. It is an older school. The community surrounding the high school has changed somewhat, but there are a large number of students whose parents attended the high school years before. The school does tend to heavily emphasize football. The rivalry from the case study is decades old, and the high school has a reputation as choice recruiting ground for college football teams. As with many larger schools, violent incidents are not uncommon. The school had many fights each year, but very few incidents with weapons. The school has a full-time police officer, and students face criminal charges for fighting in addition to school sanctions.

The Players

Mrs. Ogden had been a rebellious teenager. She had disagreed with her parents on everything. What she had wanted more than anything was to leave them and the small town behind. And she did. After fighting with her parents for four years of high school, Mrs. Ogden had moved across the country to California to attend college. Through different classes and service projects, she found she enjoyed teaching and interacting with adolescents. She found a subject she enjoyed and pursued a teaching certificate. After graduation, she moved to the Midwest with her fiancé and began a new life. She has been teaching at this school since that time. Five years ago, her husband died in a hunting accident and Mrs. Ogden was left alone. She has no children and she is an only child. Not too long after her husband's death, her mother was diagnosed with Alzheimer's and needed supervision. Mrs. Ogden's father had passed away years earlier so she moved her mother across the country into an apartment. Since then her mother had deteriorated and lived with Mrs. Ogden and is now in need of full-time care. All of this has led Mrs. Ogden to reflect on her life and relationships. She is under a great deal of stress and is very emotional. For the first time in her career her personal life may be affecting her teaching.

Steven is the all-American high school football player. Not only is Steven well known and well liked in school, but he is also well liked by the parents and community. Steven was raised in a Christian home by two parents. He has a younger brother who is eight years old. Both of his parents work. His father is a teacher and his mother works in the church office. Steven never gets into trouble at school. He is an average student and an average football player. His real gift in life is writing. He writes short stories and cartoons and hopes to pursue it in college. Although Steven is mild mannered and well behaved, he is like any other person—he has his limits to what he will tolerate. Unfortunately, Brad pushed Steven past those limits.

Brad has been raised with little respect for the laws of the state or country. His family was rather well off until his father became overwhelmed with gambling debt. His father is a local lawyer and his mother does not work outside the home. He has three younger sisters. Following his father's example, Brad looks for the easy way to make a buck or grade in life. Brad also feels he and his family are exempt from the laws that govern the other people in the state. For example, Brad helped his father set fire to their lake house in order to collect on the insurance. Brad rationalizes they are beating the system and cannot see any moral or ethical problems in his family's behavior. Brad continually gets in minor trouble in school, but he has managed to avoid any major incident that would lead to expulsion. Brad is very bright, but unfortunately uses his intelligence for scamming and avoiding confrontations with authority. Steven's example as a stellar student irritates Brad to no end.

THINGS TO CONSIDER

Discussion Questions

1. In this scenario, do you think it was within the control of Mrs. Ogden to prevent a fight from occurring? Why or why not? If so, what could she have done differently to prevent a fight?
2. In your opinion, what factors in the classroom environment contributed to the fight?
3. No one wants a fight to occur in his or her classroom. By creating a safe and welcoming atmosphere the teacher can lessen the chances of a violent confrontation in the classroom. What are some ways a teacher can establish a safe environment in the classroom?
4. In the scenario, Mrs. Ogden's choice of response to the fight was ineffective. What are more effective strategies for managing a fight between students?
5. In most cases, schools have consequences for fighting on campus. However, it may be necessary to also have consequences for the violent students in your own classroom. What are some logical consequences that could be imposed for fighting?

Areas for Reflection

The following concepts, theories, and strategies may offer some insight into the case study. It is worth exploring the effects these ideas would have on classroom management issues.

Severe clause. Although fights in the classroom are less common than fights before or after school or between classes, it is still important to prepare for such an eventuality. Canter and Garrison (1994) discusses the use of a severe clause as part of a discipline plan. A severe clause is used when students exhibit behavior that causes the business of learning to stop in the classroom. Fighting is one example. The severe clause allows for a teacher to forego the established classroom consequences for misbehavior and immediately remove the student from the classroom. If a severe clause is made part of the classroom management plan from the beginning of school, then the students are aware that some behaviors will lead to immediate removal, and they know which behaviors those are from the start. A severe clause can help the teacher set clear expectations for behavior early in the year.

Classroom environment. Another possible way to avoid violent confrontations in the classroom is to purposefully create a classroom environment that is safe and welcoming for all students. In previous chapters, ways to connect to your students were examined. Other methods and strategies for creating a sense of community are related here. Drawing on many different studies and research projects, Larivee (2005) lists several strategies that can be used to enhance and promote a sense of community in the classroom. The following is a sample:

- Implement morning announcements or rituals such as a moment to share news or a time to discuss a quote of the day.
- Have students interview each other with questions the class has created and share the results.
- Allow for times for students to get to know each other. Any number of "getting acquainted" games will work.
- Have a place or space for students to say nice things about each other.

Most importantly, teachers who want to create a sense of community in the classroom should model respect and sincerity in student-teacher interactions. Students will treat others how they are treated.

Stages of fights. If, unfortunately, a fight occurs in the classroom, it is useful to know how a typical physical confrontation progresses. According to Canter and Garrison (1994), there are three stages of a student fight: escalation, intense fighting, and the lull. In the first stage, escalation, students exchange aggressive verbal insults and comments. In this stage, Canter and Garrison offers a few strategies to end the conflict:

- Make loud diverting sounds;
- Use short, clear commands;
- Identify the victim;
- Set reasonable and enforceable limits;
- Follow through with consequences. (p. 67)

Stage two, intense fighting, is the time when the participants begin physical attacks. It is usually fairly difficult for an individual to break up a fight in this stage. Please consider the risks before intervening. Canter and Garrison offers the following strategies:.

- Send for backup at once;
- Use short, clear commands;
- Remove the audience;
- Remove potentially harmful objects. (p. 68)

Finally, after thirty to sixty seconds of intense fighting, the combatants will enter the lull or final stage. Canter and Garrison suggests:

- Use short clear commands;
- Separate the combatants;
- Get assistance. (p. 69)

Teachers need to remember that anytime they intervene in a physical confrontation there is potential for harm to come to them either intentionally or unintentionally. Obviously, the safest times to intervene in a confrontation are the escalation stage or the lull. Hopefully, few teachers will actually face this situation in their careers.

ROLE-PLAY IDEAS

Cast Study Cast: Mrs. Ogden, Steven, Brad, and two to five other students

1. Have students act out the entire scenario with dialogue, carefully. Afterwards, have students discuss how Mrs. Ogden could have intervened at different times and let them act out each idea. Then discuss which is most effective.
2. Have students act out various strategies for Mrs. Ogden to implement with the fighters as the confrontation ends. Discuss which are more effective.
3. In small groups, have students brainstorm ways Mrs. Ogden could have avoided the confrontation. Have each group act out one strategy and discuss which would be most effective.
4. Have students act out what could possibly happen between Mrs. Ogden and the students in class the next school day. Discuss what effects the fight would have on the classroom climate.

⓭

BULLIES

In the past few years, the media have spotlighted the issue of bullying in many news shows. However, the phenomenon of bullying is not new and will not ever be completely erased from our social landscape. There are bullies in the global world as there are in schools. In schools, educators need to be aware of bullies in order to redirect the behavior, teach appropriate social interactions, and protect possible victims. No student should have to attend school in fear of being a victim of an aggressor. The following case explores an incident of bullying in the secondary education classroom.

THE SCENARIO

The seventh-grade science fair was only one week away and Mr. Simpson was stressed. He had 174 students working on 47 different science fair projects. This year he let students work with partners because managing 169 projects last year nearly cost him his marriage. Still, it was a lot to oversee, and the students were getting anxious about the competition as well. Most of the projects were in good shape and the topics ranged from paper chromatography to crop soil comparisons. The students had today, Tuesday, and tomorrow to finish the final report and hand it in. Then on Thursday and Friday, the students would create the presentation boards and materials. On Monday, the class would be open to the school and community for viewing of the projects, and the science fair was next Tuesday.

Mr. Simpson was divided; he loved the excitement of the students as they prepared results, but he hated the chaos of the week before the fair. It was his most anticipated and dreaded time of year. This year he felt he had managed the whole process more effectively than years before. All he had to do was make it to Tuesday.

The morning classes went smoothly if you could call well-managed chaos smooth. By lunch, Mr. Simpson was ready for a break. He ate with his friend Mr. Ellis in the teacher's lounge and talked about their upcoming camping trip. Mr. Simpson was relaxed and happy as fifth period started after lunch. As the students filed through the door, Mr. Simpson smiled and greeted each one. Finally, everyone was seated and Mr. Simpson started class.

"Afternoon, everyone. Does anyone have news or announcements?" Mr. Simpson began.

"I do," Sally said. "My dog Lady had five puppies last night. If anyone wants one, let me know."

"Thanks, Sally. Anyone else? No? Okay. Let's get to it. Today we are going to finish compiling the data from your projects and put that information together in a research report format. The format is on the board, and you have a handout in your science fair packet. Your report is due to me by the end of class tomorrow. You have the rest of the period to work with your partner. I will be checking with each group throughout class. Any questions? No? Okay. Get to work," Mr. Simpson said.

The students moved off in pairs to begin work. The class was somewhat noisy as everyone was talking and working. Mr. Simpson didn't mind the noise because it made him feel like his students were productive. Mr. Simpson began his informal progress checks of each group. About ten minutes into working, the noise of the class changed. Mr. Simpson heard a loud voice rise above the excited chatter of the class. He looked around but could not tell to whom the voice belonged.

"Okay. Everybody needs to make sure they are on task. Keep up the good work," Mr. Simpson directed.

Jenn and Jasmine were talking as they worked on their projects. Basically, they were through with the report and were already working on the signs and letters for the presentation board. At the table next to them, Nancy and Cindy were working on their reports.

"Hey, Jasmine, that looks great. I really like the . . ." Jenn paused. "Do you smell something?" she whispered.

Jasmine smelled the air. "Yeah. That stinks. What is it?"

Jenn looked for the source of the smell. "Oh my god. It's Cindy. She stinks!"

"You're right. That is so gross. What is her problem?" Jasmine said.

The girls completely stopped worked and began to talk louder and louder. As their voices grew in volume, the work that Cindy and Nancy were doing slowly declined until all they were doing was listening to Jenn and Jasmine.

"I can't believe anyone could smell that bad," Jenn said.

"Tell me. Does she not own a washcloth? I mean even if she is poor, she can use some soap and water," Jasmine said.

"Ugh. I can't do any work here. I think I am going to throw up," Jenn said.

Nancy had heard enough. "Hey, why don't you two shut up and get to work."

Jasmine turned to Nancy and Cindy. "Hey, Nancy, we know you can't help it that she's your partner. I don't know how you can stand it. You can come work with us if you want," she said.

By now Cindy was horrified and visibly upset. She was cringing with every word and tried to stay behind Nancy so she wouldn't have to face the girls. She had never felt so ashamed and humiliated.

And, then as if motivated by Cindy's discomfort and pain, Jenn and Jasmine launched a full-blown verbal attack.

"Hey, Cindy! I can still see your fat butt! You can't hide behind Nancy. You're too fat and wide. Get your fat stinking butt over here and quit hiding like a baby," Jenn said.

"We know you're stinky and fat, but you are also stupid and ugly. Didn't anyone tell you how to take care of yourself? You need to wash!

Look at your greasy stringy hair," Jasmine said as she roared with laughter.

"Come over here and tell us why you're so stinky and gross. Do you need some soap at home? Are you too poor to buy soap?" Jenn taunted.

Finally, Cindy had reached her breaking point and she let out a loud wail and burst into sobs falling to the floor. Mr. Simpson ran over to her.

"Cindy, are you okay? Are you hurt?" he asked. He was always worried about someone getting hurt in lab.

Cindy could not answer. "She's not hurt. Jenn and Jasmine were saying mean things to her," Nancy said.

Mr. Simpson looked at Cindy on the floor. "What kinds of mean things were they saying?" he asked.

"They told Cindy she stinks and is ugly," Nancy answered for Cindy.

Mr. Simpson looked at the two girls. "Did you really say that to her?"

"Mr. Simpson, you know she stinks. We were just trying to help her," Jenn said.

Mr. Simpson could not believe his ears. He looked at the girls dumbfounded. "Jenn and Jasmine, please go sit at my desk until I decide what to do with you."

Jenn and Jasmine left. Mr. Simpson turned to Cindy on the floor still crying. He knew he must do something, but crying girls were not his strong point.

"Cindy, come on. Stop crying. Everything is going to be all right." Then he had an idea. "Let's go down and talk with the counselor. Nancy can go with you."

Cindy looked at Mr. Simpson and Nancy and managed to slow her tears to sniffles as she got up off the floor.

As Cindy and Nancy left, Mr. Simpson again wondered about the savage qualities of adolescent girls. How could anyone ever understand them?

BACKGROUND INFORMATION

The School

The school is a large urban middle school. The student population is diverse in terms of gender, religion, and ethnicity. However, the most diverse characteristic of the school is the continuum of economics. The school serves an area that houses very wealthy families and very poor families. There are a majority of poor students in the school, but there are a large number of upper middle-class families also. The school has tried to promote appreciation of different cultures by using multicultural education and other strategies. Unfortunately, like many other schools, the administration has overlooked the diverse economic backgrounds of its students and the tensions and issues that diversity can create.

The Players

Mr. Simpson has been teaching for six years. This is his second year at his current school. For his first four years, Mr. Simpson taught in an inner-city school in the North as an obligation to his scholarships. He moved to his new school after he was married. He and his wife are living in her hometown. His wife is a first-grade teacher in the same district. They are young, newly wed, and still very eager teachers. They hope to start a family soon. Mr. Simpson has a deep respect for science and hopes to instill that in his students. He also enjoys teaching at the middle school level. Mr. Simpson's one weakness is that he cannot foresee problems with lessons or discipline in his classroom. Each time a major incident occurs, he is caught off guard. On the bright side, Mr. Simpson realizes this is his weakness and continues to work on it.

Jenn lives with her father and stepmother who are upper middle class. Her dad is an orthodontist and her stepmother is a painter. Jenn's mother left her with her father when she was three and she hasn't seen her since. Her dad remarried when Jenn was five. Jenn doesn't get along very well with her stepmother. She feels her stepmother is more interested in Jenn's two half-brothers than her. Jenn rarely sees her father. When he is not working, he is off hunting or camping or hiking. Many times he takes the boys, but never Jenn. In school, Jenn is popular and charming, most of the time. At school she looks for the attention she misses at home. Usually this need for attention is positively manifested, but lately she has been looking for any kind of attention.

Jasmine is the oldest sibling of three girls. Her parents are still married and are middle class. Jasmine's family does not make the kind of money Jenn's does. Her father works in the construction business and her mother does not work outside the home. She is home to send the older girls off to school and take care of their four-year-old during the day. Jasmine is not as popular as Jenn, but she has found a way into the popular circle by following Jenn's lead and mimicking her style and attitude. Jasmine desperately wants to be well liked and is constantly afraid someone may see her for who she really is. What Jasmine doesn't realize is who she really is is far better than who she is pretending to be.

Cindy lives with her mother and two younger siblings. Cindy's father was a construction worker who ran off with a waitress from the local diner several years ago. Before he left, the family was living paycheck to paycheck, but not lacking for any essentials. He left Cindy's mother when Cindy was six, her brother was four, and her sister was two. The first two years were not that hard. Cindy's grandmother took them in and watched the small children while Cindy's mother worked and Cindy went to school. Then her grandmother died. Cindy's mother became depressed and began drinking, and Cindy became the primary caregiver to her brother and sister. Her mother works intermittently as a waitress and receives some assistance from the state. Yet there have been times the electricity, phone, and water utilities were cut off due to nonpayment. Cindy is trying her best to be a good daughter, sister, and surrogate mother. Obviously, succeeding in school is important to her future, but fitting in with peers is a luxury she can't afford.

THINGS TO CONSIDER

Discussion Questions

1. What are some ways teachers can prevent students from bullying each other in the classroom?
2. Was there any time when Mr. Simpson could have stopped the incident from occurring or escalating? If so, when and how?
3. When dealing with bullying, it is not only important to address the behavior of the bully but it is also critical to tend to the needs of the victims. What are ways teachers can discipline the bully and help the victim at the same time?

4. Students are chosen as victims of ridicule and taunting for numerous reasons. Based on your experience, what are some reasons students get bullied? How does this information help a teacher?
5. Bullying is a social issue; it is not a problem that arises due to the curriculum. However, there may be ways in which teachers can integrate nonbullying lessons or topics into the curriculum of their classes. What are some examples of ways to accomplish this in each subject area?

Areas for Reflection

The following concepts, theories, and strategies may offer some insight into the case study. It is worth exploring the effects these ideas would have on classroom management issues.

Effects of bullying. The concept of bullying has drawn a significant amount of research. Several studies have related the long-term effects of being bullied. Students are not only affected for the time of the bullying incident but also throughout their early adult if not throughout life. Olweus (2003) lists some effects of being bullied as:

- A depressive attitude;
- A tendency toward negative self-image;
- Low self-confidence;
- Few or no friends (p. 14, p. 24).

Limber (1997) states that bullied students can become depressed and lose interest in school. For a time, bullying was considered to be a normal part of adolescence. Today, bullying is viewed as a serious social issue with dire consequences. The victims of bullies have real and serious lasting effects from the experience.

Characteristics of victims. Although any student can be singled out for bullying, certain students are at higher risk for becoming victims of bullies. Canter and Garrison (1994) state there is a higher risk of becoming a victim for students who are:

- Physically weak and cannot defend themselves;
- Passive and do not stick up for themselves;

- Socially isolated and spend most of their out-of-class time alone;
- Physically handicapped, learning disabled, or have compromised intellectual function. (p. 76)

By no means will all of these students become the victims of bullies in school, but these groups of students in general run a higher risk of being chosen as targets. Teachers need to be aware of which students in their classes could possibly be targets for a bully.

Strategies for dealing with bullies.   Teachers must take a proactive approach to prevent bullying behavior. There are strategies for teachers and students to use to combat bullying behavior. Canter and Garrison (1994) list ways teachers can confront bullying behavior:

- Bring the issue out into the open;
- Set clear expectations;
- Implement consequences;
- Be an active presence;
- Teach students how to resist bullies;
- Guide bullies toward pro-social behavior;
- Teach students to assist each other;
- Support schoolwide efforts to reduce bullying behavior. (pp. 76–80)

Many instances of bullying in the classroom can be prevented by teachers becoming aware of bullying behaviors and closely monitoring the social interactions of the classroom. Teachers can also enlist students to help stop bullies by encouraging them to follow the strategies suggested by Beane (1999, p. 115–144):

- Refuse to join or watch bullying;
- Speak out;
- Report any bullying they witness;
- Stand up for the victim of the bully;
- Include students who are normally left out;
- Distract the bully.

Bullying is a social issue and can be minimized by incorporating pro-social behaviors into the classroom. Teachers can make a difference by

openly addressing and discussing bullying in their classes and supporting students to act appropriately.

ROLE-PLAY IDEAS

Case Study Cast: Mr. Simpson, Jenn, Jasmine, Cindy, Nancy, and two to
five other students

1. Have students act out the entire scenario with dialogue. Have the
   student portraying Mr. Simpson try a few strategies in dealing with
   Cindy or Jenn and Jasmine. Discuss what is effective.
2. In small groups, have students brainstorm ways to deal with Jenn
   and Jasmine. Have each group act out one strategy. Discuss which
   ones are most effective.
3. In small groups, have students brainstorm ways to deal with Cindy.
   Have each group act out one strategy. Discuss which ones are most
   effective.

WEAPONS

Every teacher's worst fear today is to be confronted by a weapon at school or in class. Media coverage of violent incidents at schools has left teachers and students feeling that schools are unsafe, which may or may not be the case. Although the odds of a violent incident occurring in the classroom are small, it is, nevertheless, important to think about what a teacher should do in an armed confrontation with a student. The following scenario sets up one possibility for facing a student with a weapon in the classroom.

THE SCENARIO

Mrs. Lester was happy that is was the last class of the day. Today was Wednesday and she couldn't wait until the weekend. Mrs. Lester is the drama teacher for a small town school. Next Thursday is the opening of their fall play, "Our Town." She has a rehearsal tonight and tomorrow night, and then the weekend to relax before the chaos of opening a show sets in on Monday. Although she is tired and overwhelmed with final loose ends to tie up for the play, she is very dedicated to making sure her drama students still receive well-planned and engaging instruction in class. She does not think it is fair to take time away from classroom instruction to prepare for an extracurricular event. So, today Mrs. Lester plans on continuing her lecture about Elizabethan theater. She will finish her lecture notes this week, and the students will begin rehearsing scenes and monologues from the time period next week. Mrs. Lester loves theater history and she thinks the students pick up on that and in turn are more focused. After all, to most students, history is boring and theater history even more so. Luckily, all the classes have paid attention and stayed on task today. Just one more class to go.

The class came in and there was a lot of talk about the play next week. Mrs. Lester got her lecture materials together and began class.

"Hello, guys. I know you are all excited about the play next week, but we really need to focus on theater history for a little bit today. We don't want to get behind. Let's get out your notes and get ready," Mrs. Lester said.

"I have a question, Mrs. Lester," Miranda said.

"What is it?" Mrs. Lester said.

"Well, if we are not in the play and we go see it, can we get extra credit?" Miranda asked.

"Well, I hadn't really thought about it." Mrs. Lester took a minute to decide. "I think that I can't give you extra credit for just showing up, but if you went to the play then wrote a one-page review of the play, then I could give you up to ten points based on the quality of your work. How does that sound?" Mrs. Lester said.

"That's cool," Miranda said as the class agreed.

"Okay. Let's see where we left off yesterday. Oh, here we are. We were talking about characteristics of the Globe theater in England. Can anybody remember why the Globe theater is important?" Mrs. Lester asked.

"That's the place where they did Shakespeare's plays," Cathy answered.

"Great. That's right. The Globe theater was the venue for many of Shakespeare's plays. Now let's talk a little about the structure of the building itself," Mrs. Lester said as someone knocked on the door. "Paul, answer that."

Paul stood up and answered the door. A student Mrs. Lester did not recognize was standing there. Paul asked him what he needed.

"I need to see Cathy," the student replied.

"Do you have a note from the office or a hall pass?" Mrs. Lester asked from her lectern.

"I just need to talk to her for a minute," the visitor said.

Something struck Mrs. Lester as odd. She walked over to the door to talk to the student. "We are in the middle of class and unless you have an official reason for interrupting, you will have to go," Mrs. Lester said.

"Ain't you gonna let me talk to her?" the boy asked.

"No. Now please leave," Mrs. Lester said.

"Fine. I see how you are," the student mumbled as he turned.

As Mrs. Lester turned to make her way back to the front of the class, she saw Paul standing there. "Who was that?" she whispered.

"That was Donald Berryman. I think he is Cathy's ex-boyfriend," Paul said.

As Mrs. Lester continued the lesson, she wrote down the student's name to give to the principal after school. She wondered how he was able to roam around without anyone stopping him. She looked at Cathy who appeared nervous and quite uncomfortable. Maybe she should call the office now.

"Okay, guys. I need to make a quick call to the office. I want you to look in your text for the structural characteristics of the Globe," Mrs. Lester said.

She went to her desk and dialed the office. Linda, the principal's secretary, answered and took down the name and a brief description of the incident. As she was hanging up, someone knocked on the door again. Thinking it was the principal, Mrs. Lester moved to answer the door herself.

Just then the door opened and there was Donald.

"I decided I was going to talk to Cathy after all. You can't stop me," Donald said.

"Well, Donald, you are interrupting our class. We are trying to get some work done. I am sure Cathy will be willing to talk to you after school," Mrs. Lester said.

"No. I'm gonna talk to her now. Cathy, come here," Donald yelled.

"I don't want to," Cathy said.

Mrs. Lester had no idea what was going on between the two teenagers, but it was clear Cathy was scared and needed help.

"You may not talk to her. Leave the class now," Mrs. Lester said as she moved toward Donald.

Suddenly, Donald reached in his front pocket and pulled out a small black handgun and pointed it directly at Mrs. Lester. "You better shut up and back up. Or I will shoot you. Then I will talk to Cathy."

Mrs. Lester had never been so scared in her whole life. She was afraid for her safety, but even more for the safety of her students. She tried to think about what they had told her to do in this situation. She came up blank. Hadn't anyone told her what to do when faced with a student with a gun?

"Okay. Donald, I think we can let you talk to Cathy for a minute, but I will have to have the gun first," Mrs. Lester said improvising.

Donald began shaking his head. "Just give Cathy to me and I will go," he said.

Donald was standing in the middle of the classroom with his back to the door. Therefore, he couldn't see Paul slip out of the door and run for help.

Meanwhile, Mrs. Lester tried to keep talking to Donald in a calm manner, but he was still angry and would not back down from his demand to take Cathy. Mrs. Lester knew that if it came down to her or Cathy, she would not have a choice. It occurred to Mrs. Lester that this was really happening and she may not be alive tomorrow to see if all the students made it through.

As soon as she ran out of things to say, she saw Paul, the principal, and the school police officer in the door. In a matter of seconds, they had Donald on the floor.

BACKGROUND INFORMATION

The School

The school where Mrs. Lester is employed serves a small town and its community. This high school has a population of 900 students. It is the only high school in the district. The community is rather isolated from urban influences as the closest large city is over two hours away. There is no history of gang violence, racial tensions, or extreme poverty. The school is not extraordinary in any sense. The test scores are close to the national average, and the teachers do a good job of meeting the needs of all their students. Overall, there is not one characteristic or trait that one could flag for a possible violent incident to occur here.

The Players

Mrs. Lester has been teaching for 12 years. She is married to a local pharmacist and they have two boys aged eight and six. Mrs. Lester has always been involved in theater and found that teaching high school is rewarding and works well with her family schedule. Mrs. Lester struggled for the first few years against the notion held by students that theater arts should be a blow-off class, but now students come to class expectant and eager. She has made it clear that she has high expectations for her students, but will not ask for more than they can give. She is popular with the students and well liked among the teachers. In fact, she was awarded teacher of the year for the district last year.

Donald is a disturbed 16 year old. Donald lives alone with his father who spends time in the county jail on a regular basis mostly for drinking and assault. When his father is locked up, Donald takes care of himself. He cannot remember his mother; she died when he was two. There have been a string of women who have lived with them, but lately his father has preferred the bottle over the company of women. Right now, Donald's father has been gone for two weeks. He was left with no money and only has his minimum wage check from his after school job to pay for food and necessities. He doesn't know how he will pay rent in another week. Cathy and Donald had been going together for a month. Cathy knew Donald from school and had never visited his home or knew anything about his family. Basically, they spent time at school and at her house. After a month, Cathy decided she did not want to be serious and broke up with Donald. That was two days ago. Donald has been trying to contact her and she has refused. In addition, Donald's best friend moved to another state. Donald is alone and scared and angry. And no one knows it.

THINGS TO CONSIDER

Discussion Questions

1. What are some strategies or procedures that Mrs. Lester could implement to lessen the likelihood of an incident like this one from occurring (i.e., keeping the door locked from the outside)?
2. Once a weapon has been introduced in the incident, what is Mrs. Lester's primary responsibility? What should her next step be?
3. Students do bring guns to school, although having a gun drawn in your classroom should be highly unlikely. However, students can also use other items in the classroom as weapons. What are some items that could be used dangerously in a classroom? What should the procedures be to use these items and store them?
4. Most schools now have police officers for the district. What is the role of the police on a school campus? How does a teacher use the resources of the police?
5. At the end of the case, help arrives. In a worst-case scenario, no one would come. What can a teacher do alone in the classroom with an armed student?

Areas for Reflection

The following concepts, theories, and strategies may offer some insight into the case study. It is worth exploring the effects these ideas would have on classroom management issues.

Overview of school violence. With all the media attention turned to violent crimes at schools, it is hard to accurately assess the threat of violence on any given campus. Each year the government publishes *Indicators of School Crime and Safety.* According to the 2004 report, between 1993 and 2003 the percentage of students carrying guns to school decreased from 12 percent to 6 percent (DeVoe et al., 2004, p. 38). Also the report found that males are more than twice as likely to carry a weapon to school, but there was no difference between racial groups (black, white, Hispanic, Asian, and Pacific Islander) in the likelihood of carrying a weapon to school (p. 38). The report also indicates that from July 1, 1999 to June 30, 2000, there were thirty-two violent deaths (homicides and suicides) at school. This would account for less than one homicide or suicide of a student at school per million students enrolled for the 1999–2000 school year (p. 6). From July 1, 1998 to June 30, 2002, there has been a decrease in the number of homicides at school, down from thirty-three deaths in 1998–1999 to fourteen during 2001–2002 (p. 6). The report continues in great detail. (A full version of the report can be downloaded at http://nces.ed.gov.)

Reduction strategies. There are many things individual teachers can implement to reduce the possibility of a violent incident occurring in the classroom. Also, many school districts have implemented campuswide programs to combat possible violence on campus. According to Charles (2005), there are four main approaches schools have implemented to deal with violence including zero tolerance policies, increased school security, formal violence prevention programs, and programs in character education and conflict resolution (p. 267). The first two strategies are designed to stop a possible incident from occurring, while the second two are focused more on teaching students alternative methods for coping with anger and emotions that may lead to a violent incident. On the individual level, Canter and Garrison (1994) offer the following suggestions for teachers:

- Provide students with praise;
- Interact with students on a personal level;
- Attend student events;
- Drop notes to students;
- Initiate special programs you are interested in (i.e., photography club);
- Set up an adopt-a-student program. (pp. 97–98)

When talking about violence at school, it is more important to focus on the prevention of such incidents rather than emergency plans for what do when an incident occurs.

Strategies for a violent incident. Having just stated that prevention is more important than an emergency plan, it is foolhardy not to think about ways to address a violent situation. What is a teacher supposed to do when a student pulls a gun? Canter and Garrison (1994) offer some suggestions:

- Remain calm;
- Use appropriate motions, including turning your body sideways to protect organs, stepping backwards, and lowering your hands to a nonthreatening position;
- Protect the other students by clearing the area;
- Reassure the assailant by offering ways out of the situation;
- Get help. (pp. 70–71)

Once a student has a weapon in the classroom, the role of the teacher is to keep the situation from escalating. By remaining calm, teachers who have been in situations like these with armed students have been able to successfully resolve the situation with no injuries. Hopefully, no teacher will face this type of situation, but by thinking of possible strategies and plans, teachers can be prepared.

ROLE-PLAY IDEAS

Case Study Cast: Mrs. Lester, Donald, Cathy, and two to five other students

1. Have students act out the entire scenario with dialogue. Have the student portraying Mrs. Lester try a few strategies in dealing with Donald before he draws a gun. Discuss what is effective in preventing the incident.
2. In small groups, have students brainstorm ways to deal with Donald after he has returned with the gun. Have each group act out one strategy. Discuss which ones are most effective.
3. In small groups, have students brainstorm ways to talk with the class after the incident has occurred. Have each group act out one strategy. Discuss which ones are most effective in reassuring the students and returning the class to a normal learning environment.

AN ANGRY PARENT

Sometimes it is not a student who instigates a classroom disruption. People *outside* the classroom environment can also cause a problem *in* the classroom. Although it is not an everyday occurrence, angry parents of students will visit schools in order to confront their child's teacher about the issue. Most of the time visitors have to sign in at the office and are announced to teachers. However, it is possible for a parent or visitor to simply show up at the classroom door. This case describes an incident with an irate parent arriving unannounced at the classroom door.

THE SCENARIO

Mr. Blanton taught twelfth-grade English in a small town that revolved around basketball. This was his first year to teach and he was still very excited starting the second half of the school year. Before the holiday break, Mr. Blanton felt tired and stressed, but he had a nice vacation with his fiancée and her family and now feels rested and reenergized.

Yesterday was the first day back after the holiday break and things went well. Mr. Blanton introduced the unit on research, and students began to discuss ideas for their senior research projects. He was pleasantly surprised

by some of the ideas they came up with. Yesterday was also the day grades
came out for the fall semester. Students can log on to the school's website
and view their grades, but many don't have access to the Internet so paper
copies are also distributed.

Mr. Blanton has mixed feelings about report cards and grades that he
cannot seem to resolve. He knows that it is important to have a summative evaluation of a student's work, but he still feels that grades can be
arbitrary at times. His district requires ten daily grades and two test
grades per six-week period. Mr. Blanton still struggles with creating
daily assessments that are reliable and valid. He feels good about his
summative assessments; he tries to create authentic and performance
assessments for each grading period. Still, he isn't sure if he has the
grading system down yet. His class percentages for 170 students break-
down as follows:

A = 46%
B = 31%
C = 19%
F = 4%

Basically the only students who fail Mr. Blanton's class are those students who refuse to participate. He can't remember failing anyone for
substandard work, just incomplete or missing work. He just isn't sure he
is doing it right.

On the other hand, Mr. Blanton has made a tremendous effort to
reach out to the students who are failing at midpoint so they can make
up work and catch up. Since he started teaching, he has called the parents of each student who is in danger of failing the grading period. That
is what he learned in college and it seems to be working. Most of the
parents are very nice and appreciative of the notice. In fact, the number
of students failing at midpoint is higher than the number of students
who actually fail, so he thinks he is helping. For this last reporting period, he called 20 parents and only seven students actually failed.

Mr. Blanton's school places a heavy emphasis on sports, especially
basketball. Due to this intense focus, Mr. Blanton tracks the grades of
basketball players. For this grading period, four basketball players were
failing at midpoint and two failed for the grading period. Mr. Blanton

called all of the parents and alerted the coaches and students. If a student athlete fails a class, he or she will not be eligible to participate in the sport for the following grading period until the grade is passing. Based on the last set of grades, two senior basketball players will not be eligible to play because they failed Mr. Blanton's class.

Mr. Blanton has been worrying about all of these issues over the holiday break. But, yesterday went well and there were no complaints from the students or their coaches. He thinks he can relax and focus on the upcoming research projects.

The bell rang for second period and the students ambled in. As everyone takes their seats, Mr. Blanton checked roll and gave instructions for today's activity.

"All right, girls and boys. Today we are going to continue brainstorming ideas for research projects. I want you to get into your peer groups and take five minutes to brainstorm topics for a persuasive research paper, then we will compile those and discuss them as a class. Go!" Mr. Blanton said.

Mr. Blanton was checking on each group when there was a sharp knock on the door as it opened. Mr. Blanton looked up to see a large woman in a pair of jeans and a New York Yankees sweatshirt standing in the doorway. He had no idea who she was.

"Uh, can I help you?" Mr. Blanton asked as he crossed toward the unannounced visitor.

"Are you that no-good teacher that failed my boy?" the woman asked.

"I don't really know who you are referring to. I'm Mr. Blanton. And you are?" Mr. Blanton asked, struggling to be polite.

"I'm Chris Coleman's momma. Are you the teacher that failed him?" she asked again.

The entire class was watching as Mr. Blanton tried to gain control of the situation. "I am Chris's English teacher and I would love to discuss his performance in my class. Perhaps we could talk in the conference room?" Mr. Blanton offered.

"No. I want to know. Did you fail him?" she demanded.

"Well, I believe that Chris's performance this period was not up to his usual standard," Mr. Blanton answered, trying not to talk about a student in front of the entire class. Mr. Blanton was trying to move Mrs. Coleman back toward the hallway where they could talk in private.

"I want to know why you failed my son. He can't play basketball and you have ruined any chance of a scholarship for him. What are you going to do about it?" Mrs. Coleman asked not moving.

"I really cannot discuss this in front of my class. Will you please step into the hall and we can talk about his grade there," Mr. Coleman said gesturing toward the hall.

"Don't you even think about touching me!" Mrs. Coleman yelled.

Mr. Blanton saw Mrs. Coleman pull her arm back and form her hand into a fist. He would swear later that it all happened in slow motion, but at the moment he was frozen where he stood. About the time he regained control of his muscles, Mrs. Coleman's fist connected to his nose and there was blinding pain.

Mr. Blanton screamed.

"What you gonna do now?" Mrs. Coleman asked.

As the students stared in shock and fright, two teachers from across the hall came in accompanied by the principal and managed to lead Mrs. Coleman away.

Mr. Blanton held his handkerchief over his nose and looked at his class and thought that none of his professors had ever mentioned the fact he may have to take a punch as a teacher. What were they thinking?

BACKGROUND INFORMATION

The School

This school is a small rural school that serves an entire county. Families are mainly lower middle class and poor. Academically, the school is above the national average on standardized tests. However, few students attend college due to the expense. The majority of the college-bound seniors will attend the nearby community college and pursue a vocational degree. The few who attend a four-year institution are usually the recipients of scholarships. The school has a strong history of athletes being recruited to major universities on full scholarships.

The Players

Mr. Blanton graduated from a high school very similar to where he is currently teaching. He made decent grades, but was a star baseball player and was recruited to play for a major university. He played ball and worked on his degree. As he was nearing graduation, Mr. Blanton realized he was not going to be a professional athlete and decided to do what he loved as much as baseball—teach English. As he looked for a job, he actively pursued districts like his own high school; he thought he would feel comfortable there and be able to relate to the students. He has been very happy at the school he chose. He enjoys his subject and the environment reminds him of home. He has been dating the algebra teacher since school started, and they became engaged over the holidays. All in all, Mr. Blanton tries to be a fair and just teacher, helping all students to succeed.

Mrs. Coleman has a blind spot in her view of her son. She loves him tremendously and she worries. Chris's father works as a guard at the county jail. It is a good job, but he could have gone further in his career if he had gone to college. Mrs. Coleman desperately wants Chris to go to college and get a degree. She thinks this is the only way Chris will be able to leave the county and be successful. Mrs. Coleman also has a quick temper. She was the youngest child in a house full of brothers, and she learned to speak up and protect herself. Sometimes she is too hostile in her confrontations. Mrs. Coleman thinks Chris is smart, talented, and motivated. As with most parents, she is right, but Chris is also very interested in music and girls, to which he has been paying more attention than to school work. Chris harbors a secret dream to be a bass player in a rock band. Although Mrs. Coleman was out of line in her exchange with Mr. Blanton, her intentions stem from a desire to see her son have a better life than she has.

THINGS TO CONSIDER

Discussion Questions

1. What are some procedures or strategies Mr. Blanton could implement to prevent an unannounced visitor from entering his classroom? On a schoolwide level, what are some policies that would decrease the number of unannounced visitors in the school?
2. What are some approaches Mr. Blanton could use to calm the parent in this scenario?

3. Mr. Blanton was physically assaulted in his classroom. In your opinion, what are his options for restitution? What is his best choice in dealing with the situation?

4. The students in the class witnessed the entire exchange. How should Mr. Blanton reassure and reestablish order in the classroom?

5. Apparently, the parent was very upset about her child's grade. What methods could Mr. Blanton use to communicate more effectively with parents about the progress of their children? Keep in mind all parents do not have modern conveniences like telephones and email access.

Areas for Reflection

The following concepts, theories, and strategies may offer some insight into the case study. It is worth exploring the effects these ideas would have on classroom management issues.

Communicating with parents. Most parents want to be informed about the progress of their children in their classes. Unfortunately, due to the demands of teaching, teachers often do not contact parents until there is a significant behavioral or academic problem with the student. Every teacher should consider how he or she will communicate with parents on a regular basis. Some teachers send home weekly or monthly newsletters to inform all parents about projects and upcoming activities. Some teachers maintain websites, although not all parents have access to the Internet. Another effective strategy is to make an effort to contact each parent once a semester to share good news about his or her child. In addition, teachers need to think about how to facilitate positive and effective conferences with parents. Charles (2005) offers five strategies:

- Accept the parent without prejudice;
- Attend carefully to what the parent says;
- Appreciate the parent's efforts and support;
- Affirm the child's strengths and qualities;
- Affection for the child is made evident to the parent. (p. 211)

These positive strategies can help to create a nonthreatening and welcoming environment for the parent in a conference situation. Parents come to a conference with their own issues and preconceived ideas. Some parents may be intimidated by teachers due to negative experiences from their own school days. They may be pressed for time due to work schedules. By approaching the parent as a member of the educational team and by acknowledging their knowledge of their student, teachers can facilitate more effective conferences (Emmer, Everston, & Worsham, 2006). Overall, effective communication with parents is critical for all teachers to help ensure the success of the students, and teachers need to have a clear plan for conducting those communications with parents.

Dealing with aggressive parents.   Not all parents will be cooperative and helpful. For whatever reason, some parents may come to a teacher with a great deal of hostility. MacDonald and Healy (1999) suggest that when faced with an aggressive parent, teachers need to avoid engaging in an argument and try to remain calm for as long as possible. The authors further state that "reflective empathetic listening techniques" that validate the emotions of the parent can help decrease the hostility in that parent (p. 264). As with dealing with an upset student, the most effective approach is to use a calm voice and nonthreatening body language. If a teacher is aware that a parent may be upset or aggressive prior to the conference, he or she can ask another teacher or administrator to attend the meeting as a witness or mediator.

Assault in the workplace.   The National Center for Education Statistics includes data about violence against teachers in its *Indicators of School Crime and Safety* report. In the 2004 report, the NCES reports between 1998 and 2002, teachers were the victims of 234,000 non-fatal crimes at school, which included 144,000 thefts and 90,000 violent crimes (rape, assault, and robbery) (DeVoe, 2004, p. 32). The report also states that male teachers are more likely to be victims than females, secondary teachers are more likely to be victims than elementary teachers, and urban teachers are more likely to be victims than rural or suburban teachers (p. 32). Teachers worry about the safety of their students regularly, but teachers also need to be aware that they too can be victims of a violent crime at school.

ROLE-PLAY IDEAS

Case Study Cast: Mr. Blanton, Mrs. Coleman, and two to five other students

1. Have students act out the entire scenario with dialogue. Have the student portraying Mr. Blanton try a few strategies in dealing with Mrs. Coleman before she assaults him. Discuss what is effective in preventing the incident.
2. In small groups, have students brainstorm ways Mr. Blanton could have handled the incident differently. Have each group act out one strategy. Discuss which ones are most effective.
3. In small groups, have students brainstorm ways to talk with the class after the incident has occurred. Have each group act out one strategy. Discuss which ones are most effective in reassuring the students and returning the class to a normal learning environment.

AFTERWORD

Today classroom management remains a primary concern for preservice and in-service teachers. As students prepare for careers in education, they want practical and applicable instruction on how to manage a classroom effectively. Veteran teachers are constantly reflecting on and adjusting their classroom management practices to fit the needs of the individuals in their classrooms. Given the importance placed on classroom management from the practioners, we as educators and administrators need to provide up-to-date, relevant, and practical resources and instruction for the teachers.

The purpose of this book is to provide preservice teachers, veteran teachers, professors, and administrators a resource to begin a discussion about effective classroom management techniques and strategies. The factors that influence our classrooms are numerous. Sometimes the preservice teacher only sees a few of those factors and the possible impact in their classroom management course. By incorporating case studies, it is hoped that the range of discussion can broaden to help all teachers create and maintain an effective, productive classroom. However, education is a dynamic institution, and its attributes continue to change over time. Therefore, it is also important to look to the future. We, as educators, need to understand the effects of changes in schools on classroom management approaches, how classroom management will change in the future, and the importance of continued reflection on best practices.

CHANGES IN EDUCATION

Education is ever changing. Scholars continue to research new methods and strategies for instruction, and classroom teachers continually monitor their practices and adjust for their students. In addition, the institution of schooling changes with federal legislation, state legislation, and population trends. The following issues are just a few that may have an effect on the way classrooms are managed in the future.

Inclusion

Inclusion is not a new concept, but as we have begun creating inclusive classrooms, we have not changed the styles of classroom management. In a class with a group of homogenous students, a teacher could employ the same techniques and strategies to manage the classroom. Today, we have classrooms with a wide variety of students, and the techniques that work with one student may not be effective with others. In addition, the inclusive classroom will have students working at different rates and on different levels. This multifaceted classroom is more challenging to manage than the traditional classroom. Teachers will need to consider all aspects of inclusion in order to create a productive learning environment.

Diversity

Our country is changing demographically. We are experiencing constant growth. We have new citizens coming into the country, and the makeup of our population is changing. In our classrooms, we will have a more diverse population of students. These students will not only have different ethnicity backgrounds, but also different religions, languages, socioeconomic levels, as well as abilities. The issues of diversity are more extensive than just race and skin color. One of the major factors stratifying students today is the economic level of the families of students. All of these differences will affect how teachers manage a classroom. The needs of the students will vary based on their background and experiences. In one classroom, a teacher may have a student who cannot afford to buy food to eat breakfast and a student who is neglected by her parents who work sixty hours a week to afford a beach house. Both students have needs and issues, but they are different and will need to be handled differently. As the country continues to change, the classrooms in the schools will also reflect those changes.

Technology

Continual development in technological applications makes modern day life easier and easier. The new technology will also affect the modern day classroom. Americans today are now in constant communication with each other. The Internet and email have made information readily available to people and conversations between people instantaneous no matter where the participants are located. Parents and students can now communicate while apart during the day using cell phones and BlackBerries (handheld wireless device providing email, telephone, text messaging, and web browsing). Computers have influenced nearly every discipline in schools from English classes having students use word processing programs to vocational classes using computer-assisted drafting (CAD) programs. All of the innovations have changed the dynamics of the classroom. No longer is the student sitting at a desk taking notes, but he or she is using laptop or software program to create assignments and study aids. Teachers too are affected; grading and attendance programs have given teachers more freedom in the classroom. Obviously, with all the technological developments, the way the classroom is managed must change to accommodate the new methods in education.

High-Stakes Testing

When No Child Left Behind legislation mandated yearly testing for students, high-stakes testing became a national issue. The pressures associated with high-stakes testing can change the environment of a classroom. Some teachers feel the need to teach to the test in order to ensure acceptable test scores. This approach decreases the amount of engaging and authentic instruction, which can lead to more students exhibiting off-task behaviors. Also students feel the pressure to pass the benchmark exam, and that pressure can cause stress that will change the behavior of students in the class. At this juncture the question of whether or not high-stakes testing is effective or appropriate is moot. Schools now must participate in the testing process, and teachers need to be aware of the effects of the process on their students. The influences of the culture of high-stakes testing will shape the needs of the classroom. Teachers will have to adjust how they manage the learning environment to best facilitate student learning.

Overall, these are but a few of the many changes that will have an impact on the classroom of today and tomorrow. To ensure the success of all students in today's world, teachers need to consider the changes that are taking place that will be reflected in the classroom and implement effective classroom management strategies to meet the needs of the diverse learners.

THE FUTURE OF CLASSROOM MANAGEMENT

In addition to changes in public education, there will be changes in preservice teacher education and staff development for in-service teachers. Again, as teacher educators and administrators, we need to ask the question: How can we best prepare teachers to manage classrooms? There are two ideas that may shape the classroom management course of tomorrow—role play and online instruction.

Having a background in drama, I am a proponent for the use of role play in the classroom management course. As in many professional preparation programs, preservice teachers gain little actual experience, excluding student teaching, before entering the classroom. Even the most extensive student teaching experience may not provide the preservice teacher with a variety of situations for dealing with discipline issues in the classroom. By using role-play scenarios in the classroom management course, preservice teachers can try out strategies and approaches in a safe and contained environment. In addition, administrators may use role play with in-service teachers to promote discussion about specific discipline problems in their school and district or about general concerns teachers have about classroom management. No matter how the role play is used, whether it is in the teacher education curriculum or during staff development sessions in schools, the benefits for teachers to experience possible classroom problems and attempt to solve those problems will be tremendous.

The other factor that could change the way classroom management approaches are taught is online instruction. The advent of teaching online has implications for teacher education programs as well as staff development programs. In an effort to reach a larger student base and compete with other colleges and universities, many schools have developed online programs in teacher education. Some programs are exclusively online and never require the professor and student to meet, while others are a hybrid of traditional classes and online instruction. If a program is online, it will change the classroom management course. No longer could students be required to participate in role-play situations. However, there may be hidden benefits to an online classroom management course. Student may feel more comfortable asking questions and participating in discussions in an environment that is completely virtual. The pressure of an audience in a classroom has been removed in an online course. Students may also become more reflective since the time constraints felt in a traditional class have been removed. No matter what the benefits or drawbacks, if online instruction is the medium of instruction for the future, classroom management courses will have to be adjusted.

On the other hand, online instruction could also change the shape of staff development in the public school. Many teachers and administrators are pressed for time. Schedules are tight and there is little time left over for significant staff development. Administrators could develop and offer staff development for their faculty in an online form. Teachers could participate in relevant and practical staff development at their convenience. It is quite a challenge to plan staff development for one hundred teachers with varying schedules; an online experience does not require all teachers to be in the same place at the same time. Again, the teachers also may be more open to reflection and discussion when they have chosen the time to read and participate in the online program. All in all, the online staff development could enhance the quality and experiences of teachers in their professional development opportunities.

These two factors could change the way classroom management is taught and talked about in universities and schools. Role play can offer unique experiences to the participants as can online instruction. As methods in instruction change, so too will the style and delivery of classroom management courses and programs.

IMPORTANCE OF CONTINUED REFLECTION

With all the changes in education and society, it is critical to continue to seek ways to improve practice and instruction. The responsibility for improving our schools is shared between teacher educators, in-service teachers, administrators, researchers, and legislators. Each group has its own perspective on classroom management and can contribute to improving the practices in unique ways. However, classroom teachers and teacher educators must promote continual reflection and refinement.

Classroom teachers face an ever-changing landscape in their classrooms. In order to ensure success for all students, the methodologies and practices implemented in the class must be constantly evaluated and refined, including classroom management strategies and practices. As teachers grow as classroom managers, they should begin to collaborate with other professionals about what are the best practices for the secondary education classroom.

Teacher educators also must do their part to improve the quality of America's classrooms. These professionals must conduct and read the latest research on classroom management and help disseminate that information to preservice as well as in-service teachers. The teacher educator must also listen to the preservice and in-service teachers as they voice their concerns and problems about classroom management. Hopefully these two groups together can lead the movement to better classroom management practices.

In conclusion, classroom management remains a major issue for preservice teachers, in-service teachers, administrators, and teacher educators. The changing characteristics of U.S. education will have an impact on what will be the best practices for teachers in the future. Also, with the delivery of the instruction changing to web-based or online classes teachers may find learning about classroom management easier through better accessibility and materials. No matter what the future holds for education it is imperative for everyone involved to think continually about how we can make classrooms better, safer, and more effective learning environments for all students.

REFERENCES

Bandura, A. (1986). *Social foundations of thought and action: A social-cognitive theory*. Englewood Cliffs, NJ: Prentice-Hall.

Beane, A. L. (1999). *The bully free classroom: Over 100 tips and strategies for teachers K–8*. Minneapolis: Free Spirit.

Brown, B. B., & Lohr, M. J. (1987). Peer-group affiliation and adolescent self-esteem: An integration of ego-identity and symbolic-interaction theories. *Journal of Personality and Social Psychology, 52*, 47–55.

Canter, L., & Garrison, R. (1994). *Scared or prepared*. Santa Monica, CA: Lee Canter and Associates.

Charles, C. M. (2005). *Building classroom discipline* (8th ed.). Boston: Pearson.

DeVoe, J. F., Peter, K., Kaufman, P., Miller, A., Noonan, M., Snyder, T.D. et al. (2004). *Indicators of school crime and safety: 2004.* (NCES 2005-002/NCJ 205290). U.S. Department of Education and Justice. Washington, DC: U.S. Government Printing Office.

Emmer, E. T., Everston, C. M., & Worsham, M. E. (2006). *Classroom management for middle and high school teachers* (7th ed.). Boston: Pearson.

Fischer, L., Schimmel, D., & Stellman, L. R. (2003). *Teachers and the law* (6th ed.). Boston: Allyn and Bacon.

Gardner, H. (1993). *Multiple intelligences: Theory into practice*. New York: Basic Books.

Glatthorn, A. A. (1999). *Performance standards and authentic learning*. Larchmont, NY: Eye on Education.

Good, T. L., & Brophy, J. E. (2000). *Looking in classrooms* (8th ed.). New York: Longman.

Grossman, H. (2004). *Classroom behavior management for diverse and inclusive schools* (3rd ed.). Lanham, MA: Rowman & Littlefield.

Herman, J. L., Aschbacher, P. R., & Winters, L. (1992). *A practical guide to alternative assessment.* Alexandria, VA: Association for Supervision and Curriculum Development.

Larrivee, B. (2005). *Authentic classroom management* (2nd ed.). Boston: Pearson.

Limber, S. P. (1997). Preventing violence among school children. *Family Futures, 1,* 27–28.

Love, F. E., Henderson, D. B., & Hanshaw, L. G. (1996). Preparing preservice teachers to understand diversity in classroom management. *College Student Journal, 30,* 112–118.

MacDonald, R. E., & Healy, S. D. (1999). *A handbook for beginning teachers* (2nd ed.). New York: Longman.

National Association for Gifted Children. (2005). Frequently asked questions. Retrieved October 10, 2005, from http://www.nagc.org/index.asp?id=548.

Nieto, S. (2000). *Affirming diversity* (3rd ed.). New York: Longman.

Olweus, D. (2003). *Bullying is not a fact of life* (CMHS-SVP-0052). Washington, DC: U.S. Government Printing Office.

Rinne, C. H. (1997). *Excellent classroom management.* Belmont, CA: Wadsworth.

Ryan, K., & Cooper, J. M. (2000). *Those who can, teach* (9th ed.). Boston: Houghton Mifflin.

Santrock, J. W. (2003). *Adolescence* (9th ed.). Boston: McGraw Hill.

Slavin, R. E. (1995). *Cooperative learning* (2nd ed.). Boston: Allyn and Bacon.

Smith, B. P. (2000). Emerging themes in problems experienced by student teachers: A framework for analysis. *College Student Journal, 34*(4), 633–640.

Teaching Tolerance. (1999). *Responding to hate at school: A guide for teachers, counselors, and administrators.* Montgomery, AL: Southern Poverty Law Center.

Tomlinson, C. A. (1999). *The differentiated classroom: Responding to the needs of all learners.* Alexandria, VA: Association for Supervision and Curriculum Development.

Tomlinson, C. A. (2001). *How to differentiate instruction in mixed-ability classrooms* (2nd ed.). Alexandria, VA: Association for Supervision and Curriculum Development.

Villa, R. A., & Thousand, J. S. (2003). Making inclusive education work. *Educational Leadership, 61*(2), 19–23.

Wassermann, S. (1994). *Introduction to case method teaching: A guide to the galaxy*. New York: Teachers College Press.

Wiggins, G., & McTighe, J. (1998). *Understanding by design*. Alexandria, VA: Association for Supervision and Curriculum Development.

Wolfgang, C. H. (2001). *Solving discipline and classroom management problems* (5th ed.). New York: John Wiley and Sons.

Wong, H. K., & Wong, R. T. (1998). *The first days of school*. Mountain View, CA: Harry K. Wong Publications.

ABOUT THE AUTHOR

Amanda M. Rudolph has been an educator for ten years. She taught theater arts in public schools in Texas before moving to teacher education. She is currently an assistant professor in secondary education at Stephen F. Austin State University in Nacogdoches, Texas. Rudolph earned her Ph.D. in curriculum and instruction with an arts education emphasis from the University of Arkansas. In addition to classroom management issues, her research interests include online instruction and arts education.